Athletics for the 70's

Athletics for the 70's

A Training Manual

Denis Watts and Tony Ward

Claude Vernon

Arthur Barker Ltd
London

ISBN 0 213 16417 5

*Printed in Great Britain by
Redwood Press Limited,
Trowbridge, Wiltshire.*

Contents

Acknowledgements

The longer one is associated with a sport the more one recognises that we are all constantly learning. Therefore we gratefully acknowledge all the hundreds of people, fellow coaches and administrators, who have, over the years, positively talked athletics with us, often long into the night and who have helped us develop our own philosophy.

More individually we acknowledge more recent discussions with Morton Evans, Barry Myers and Bill Thomas, various members of the CCPR and the NPFA and Peter Matthews of the NUTS for permission to reproduce his figures on club performances.

Finally, to Miss Lena Fung of Chelsea College of Physical Education and Hong-Kong our very grateful thanks for carrying out the artwork.

Illustrations

Organisation for Schools

I

General philosophy

Whether or not a school athletics club – and that is essentially what we are concerned with in this section – is successful depends on a number of factors. Ultimately, though, the factor which supersedes all others is the enthusiasm of the teacher and in nearly all cases the degree of enthusiasm or dedication or even fanaticism of the teacher is directly proportional to the success which can be obtained; given this factor there is really little limit to what can be achieved.

Even in the smallest rural school the coach/administrator has numbers of potential athletes arriving each year which would make his club counterpart green with envy, and success at a very high level has consistently been obtained by schools in athletically remote areas like Cumberland and Westmorland, the Isle of Ely and County Antrim in Northern Ireland. Other factors must and do play a part. They are:

(1) Proximity of school ground and/or track
(2) Athletics tradition in the school
(3) Support of headmaster and the rest of the staff
(4) Other school traditions
(5) Cricket
(6) Availability of athletes for training and competition
(7) Standards and enthusiasm of other schools locally

In the final analysis, however, all these factors can be met by the right degree of enthusiasm.

The problem for the physical education teacher is how to fit everything in. Today he has to be the 'expert' on swimming, athletics, golf, tennis, yachting, acqua and sub-acqua activities and even, in some cases, sex education. The smaller the school the more the burden will

I

fall upon him and, of course, it is impossible to cope adequately with all these in depth. What usually happens is that the physical education teacher has a bias towards certain games and sports and these, quite naturally, are those at which the school becomes most successful. Often the situation is alleviated by the fact that there is a member of the academic staff who is an enthusiast for a particular sport and is willing to spend a good deal of time at it. In either case how should he or she tackle the seven factors listed above?

PROXIMITY OF SCHOOL GROUND AND/OR TRACK

Surprisingly to some people this is quite a small factor, though obviously, the closer facilities are, the less the problem. If there is a track locally that is not difficult to reach, then it is a good plan to have at least one coaching session there a week. Youngsters like to identify and they stand more chance of emulating, in their own mind, a David Bedford or an Ann Wilson, on a running track than on some bumpy grass field. What perhaps ought to be stressed here is that facilities which are away from a school serve as a nuisance and should not be used as an excuse for lack of interest.

ATHLETICS TRADITION IN THE SCHOOL

If a school already has an athletics tradition then there is little problem, but building up a tradition from scratch can be a lengthy business. Tradition is really another way of saying success over a long period of time or continued success, and the discerning athletics teacher will publicise as much as possible, within the school and outside it, every level of success that is obtained: favourable comparisons with previous years; success at the Five-Star Award; success obtained at district schools level; inter-school match results and so on. Every Monday morning in the summer term the headmaster should have something to read about school athletics as well as cricket, tennis or netball.

Mainly, though, tradition must stem from interest within the school and so the athletics teacher must add a public-relations bow to his arrow. When such interest is created it will mean that, perhaps, more people will want to take part, even at a low-performance level, and the teacher should be prepared for this.

The emphasis upon success will offend the more aesthetic who will want to see emphasis upon the, for them, important factors of the sport – the sheer delight of running, jumping and throwing. They will want to emphasize not the tape measure and stop watch, but the more lofty values – how do we make youngsters who finish a sad seventh in a heat of the 200 metres feel that they have achieved something really, how can we make them realise that athletics can be so much more, even a way of life ? Fine: such things are possible, especially within the framework of the school athletics and games lessons, but at even the most lowly competitive level in the pragmatic world of the seventies the teacher, the headmaster, the parent and the friend will want to know 'How did you do ?' rather than 'How did you feel ?'

SUPPORT OF THE HEADMASTER AND THE REST OF THE STAFF

This is obviously essential and the athletics teacher must make sure that his enthusiasm does not blind him to the academic needs of his athletes, does not too frequently encroach upon other items in the timetable, does not make too many demands upon other members of staff in terms of out-of-school officiating and that at all times his athletics team and club brings credit and occasionally kudos upon the school. Follow these criteria and the teacher will generally find enthusiasm for his ventures.

OTHER SCHOOL TRADITIONS

It should also be remembered that other out-of-school activities are taking place within the school community and that those responsible for them are just as keen and enthusiastic. Respect them, use the art of give-and-take and avoid clashes where possible. When preparing fixtures, not only study other athletics and sports fixtures but also try to avoid clashes with other club activities as well. School traditions – drama, Combined Cadet Force etc. – must be kept up even, sometimes, at the sacrifice of athletics.

CRICKET

The biggest clashes will be with cricket and the very best way to avoid situations where a boy is required for the 1st XI for the most important needle fixture of the season and to run in the County Schools Athletics Championships on the same day will be to avoid using the same boys.

3

Alternatively, if school cricket and athletics fixtures clash very rarely during the term then try to spot such clashes well in advance and discuss them with the cricket teacher. It is often the discovery of such clashes the Tuesday before the date in question that sends temperatures rising.

AVAILABILITY OF ATHLETES FOR TRAINING AND COMPETITION

In urban areas this usually presents no problem but can be a major headache in rural areas where students come in from a wide area by school buses and leave by them at the end of the afternoon session. In the latter case both students and staff are all in the school at lunchtime and training/coaching sessions can take place then. From a fixture viewpoint parents are often more than willing to help out with transport problems.

STANDARDS AND ENTHUSIASM OF OTHER SCHOOLS LOCALLY

It is not much good having the strongest athletics school in the country if the opposition locally is lamentable. Teachers will learn from experience where to go for the most worthwhile fixtures and how to blend them into school life.

The next thing that should be considered is what criteria should be followed for success. There are two categories to consider:

(1) A good all-round school with good fixtures against other schools locally
(2) Individual success at various levels of the National Schools Championships

At the one end of the scale teachers try to ensure that they have as many participants as possible in their fixtures, whilst at the other, the concentration is upon a small, elitist group aiming for success at the highest possible level. As is usual, the answer lies somewhere in compromise.

The teacher should devise a programme to ensure that the club and everyone in it has a yearly purpose. The purpose may vary: for the club to annexe a certain trophy or to win an important inter-school match; for individuals it could go from beating 30 seconds for 200 metres, *via* achieving an AAA Four-Star Award to reaching the final of the National Schools Championships. By fixing such targets for his athletes the teacher can do much to avoid the aimlessness that often creeps into athletics sessions once the summer is under way. The athletes must have a purpose to keep going right through the summer term. Of necessity, the local or district Schools Championships are held very early and for too many schools an athlete making his exit from these is also making his exit from sport for the rest of the term. By aiming at the first of our criteria the teacher can kill two birds with the one stone, for individual successes will come from having a good, all-round approach to participation and fixtures.

School athletes should be encouraged to take part in as many non-athletics activities as possible. This especially applies to the star athlete (and *every* school has one now and then) who could become very good. If he plays rugby or soccer then let him; if she plays hockey or netball then let her. Encourage keenness on dramatics, music or Christian Aid. The fall-out from school athletics is of a very high order in Britain and we must be sure that, if pupils' interest in athletics wanes, or even fades out altogether, they have other interests or pursuits to follow. Athletes, especially runners, are in great danger of becoming social outcasts, for theirs is a lonely furrow, and one which they have been at for some considerable time. At schools we have the greatest opportunity to make sure that they have a wide and diversified sporting and social background. It was interesting in 1971 to hear triple Olympic champion Peter Snell say in an interview how invaluable it had been for him to have a good tennis background before he took up athletics seriously.

In formulating his ideas for his schools athletics club or team, the teacher must consider a number of other points:

SCHOOL AWARENESS

The whole school should be aware of the activities of the athletics club *via* posters, general publicity within the school and regular announcements at school assemblies. Encourage support for both at home and away matches and for local schools' championships.

TOWN/DISTRICT AWARENESS

It is also of value to link up with the local Press to give the town or locality an awareness of the achievements of the school. In more rural areas local interest can be of a very high order. Athletics matches and school sports days are often very good public relations for the school and seem to attract more Press coverage than inter-school team games.

SELECTION OF ATHLETICS CAPTAIN

This needs careful consideration each year. Obviously the selection should fall upon someone with whom the teacher can work amicably and with whom he has a good relationship. The captain must also have the respect of the other athletes. A discerning teacher will try to spot his potential captains early on and bring them along to ensure continuity. The teacher should always select the captain.

STUDENT PARTICIPATION IN ADMINISTRATION

Experience has shown that it is unwise to let the students take on too much of the secretarial work with regard to fixtures etc. Even in universities and colleges, where it is often looked upon as a symbol of student independence, it is often badly done. In most cases senior pupils have not the time because of examination commitments, and, secondly, a good deal of training is required. There is the third point that teachers in charge of athletics at other schools may well resent corresponding with a student rather than their opposite number.

CORRESPONDENCE

Some teachers in charge of sport are notorious for their poor correspondence and even their entire lack of it. Prompt replies and early transmitting of information to other schools and associations helps to build up a reputation. An annual large box of chocolates to the school secretary or another member of the administrative staff could ensure neatly typed and well-worded correspondence.

COLOURS

The award of 'colours' varies from school to school. In general the teacher should err on the selective side in awarding colours or half-colours and should not have any set criteria for awarding them. Certainly they can serve as a great incentive to youngsters at school especially when they are not *necessarily* linked to any standard of performance.

UNIFORM

Distinctive vests and shorts will certainly add to the pleasure of the athletes and be an aid to confidence. Often a school already has a colour or colours for the winter team games and it should be easy to adapt these colours for athletic purposes. This sort of approach will encourage the athletes to buy their own track suits and other gear.

NOTICE BOARDS

When a notice board is used it should be kept well up-to-date and changed regularly to keep interest. Most school notice-boards of this type are kept in an abysmal state. It may be a good idea to allow a small committee of senior boys or girls to look after it. Such a notice board (See figure 1) should include:

(1) Fixtures
(2) Results
(3) Relevant press cuttings and photographs
(4) Ranking lists – as deep as possible. Get a potential computer-programmer to work on these
(5) Photographs and items on coaching/training hints and general athletic interest

MIXED SCHOOLS

Where schools are mixed the teachers should ensure that some fixtures, especially with the more senior pupils, are also mixed. Athletics and swimming are two of the few sports where girls and boys can compete in the same surroundings and such fixtures can emphasise a social side to a sport which does not always appear over-social.

Having planned carefully the year ahead for the school athletics team, the teacher should then consider his own role. If he or she (especially she as so few women participate in organisation) is an enthusiast, involvement outside the school itself may soon become a factor. In any case immediate contact should be made and kept with both the District Schools Athletic Association and the nearest local athletic club. This may well mean deeper involvement through to County Schools Association level and even, though the requisite years must, of course, be served, to the National Schools Association. If the teacher is a qualified coach or a non-qualified expert he may soon be drafted into

SCHOOL ATHLETICS BOARD

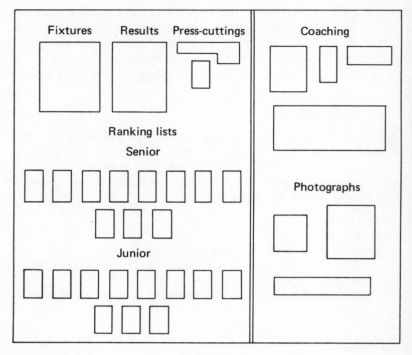

Figure 1

coaching at the local club, dealing with an ever-widening strata of athletes, and then climbing a ladder divorced from schools athletics altogether. The teacher must weigh up the sort of commitment he is being asked to make and the effect it will have on him, his family, his social life and his own school's athletics. There have been a number of cases where the standard and enthusiasm of athletics within a school has deteriorated as the teacher's involvement in athletics activities outside his own school have increased. This is not to say that the teacher should not involve himself in these activities, far from it, but he should keep a wary eye on all his commitments to make sure that he can fulfil them all adequately. In his commitment to his own school he should critically assess what time he will have available for after-school, lunch-time coaching etc., announce it at the beginning of term and stick to such a programme: e.g. Tuesday evenings and Thursday lunch-time. Don't let early term enthusiasm make the commitment one that cannot be kept. In his link up with the local club the teacher should think in terms of mutual assistance. He will know what standard of coaching he is able to achieve, and if his athletes go beyond that he should be happy to pass them on to the local club (providing an adequate standard is available there). In any case clubs can, in the main, provide a higher standard of competition for the better athletes.

The percentage of club-orientated athletes appearing in the finals of National Schools Championships is very high indeed, clearly indicating the necessity for this type of coaching and competition at that level. The teacher can also obtain a list of local club fixtures to avoid, where possible, major clashes. Many teachers are adamant that the 'school has first claim' rule should be rigidly adhered to, but a slightly more flexible approach can often produce more profitable results for all parties.

Finally the teacher must consider his own role and stance towards the enormous drop-away of schools' athletes. Much has been written on this topic in the past and it may well be that a less well-organised system of school athletics in Britain could lead to more participation at senior level as evidence from the continent seems to suggest. On the other hand, it could make no difference at all. One thing is clear at the present time: schools' athletes of whatever age must always compete to the highest peak of their ability at that time for who can know what tomorrow or the next year may bring?

2

Inter-schools fixtures

Competition is the spice of athletic life and the main spar of any school athletics club or team must be its competitive structure. There will be, in the main, two types of competition – individual and team.

INDIVIDUAL COMPETITION

The main individual competition for schools athletes is the local District Schools Championships and the structure and type of this competition will vary from area to area and county to county. In most big urban areas it will be the town or borough championship meeting whilst in more rural districts it will take the form of a sub-county meeting. Every effort should be made to have a full entry in this competition (which can also be inter-school in nature). Winners and other specified athletes go on to a county or provincial type of championship.

Other open athletic meetings are often staged as well as County AAA or County WAAA championships and appropriate athletes should be entered for such meetings. Open graded meetings and other types of competition are staged by clubs and the schools athletics teacher should be aware of these.

TEAM COMPETITION

A sound programme of inter-school matches right through the term will create interest and enthusiasm and give young athletes a taste of what athletics later in life ought to be.

TYPES OF FIXTURE

In 'friendly' inter-schools fixtures the teacher should aim at a certain amount of variety: senior fixtures; junior fixtures; senior and junior matches combined; Under-13 matches; matches involving boys' and girls' teams together. This will ensure that all of those interested in competing are catered for. Try to fix important, tough or 'needle' fixtures for the end of the summer term to ensure that the team is fully fit and prepared for the match – every school has its particular Eton versus Harrow.

In preparing fixtures try to ascertain the dates of the major inter-schools fixtures: District/Town; County/Provincial/Area; National Schools Championships, and avoid clashes in close proximity to these. Find out when both the internal and external examinations are taking place and avoid these weeks – though this does not mean a total abandonment of fixtures whilst all examinations are on. Whilst the major O and A Level or CSE examinations are taking place, junior fixtures can still be held.

In the main the dual meeting is obsolete, though one must recognise that traditional dual fixtures of many years standing have an important place in school life. If a six-lane track is available, however, a triangular fixture adds interest, is more exciting and the extra officiating involved is minimal.

In fixing the number of home matches the teacher should bear in mind that he will probably need fellow members of staff to officiate and so the willing horse should not be flogged too often on after-school fixtures.

Other ideas for fixtures are: jumps and throws matches (which need not take too long and require a minimum of officials); relay matches; Kirkby Sevens (see club competition section) and pentathlon matches based on the AAA Five-Star Award scoring tables.

FIXTURE DATES

Schools that have a series of traditional fixtures set each year provide an easy task for the teacher concerned.

For the newly appointed teacher wanting to find fixtures and for the one that wants to build up his present list, the best and quickest method is to visit the annual meeting of the District or County Schools Athletics Association where he is more likely to find fellow enthusiasts than anywhere else. In fact he or she will soon get to know the athletically conscious schools in the area and wider afield. In fact District Schools and even County Schools Associations, which seem to exist at the present time for quite limited purposes, could well stage fixture meetings for the schools in their area so that teachers can arrange their fixtures in one evening.

Sort out the dates that you would like in advance and then attend a fixtures meeting or write to your opposite numbers in other schools.

CORRESPONDENCE

Write well in advance (during the autumn term if possible); suggest a date and if writing to a new opponent, suggest age groups and events. Always have as full a programme as is possible. Keep a copy of all correspondence. Be prompt in writing and replying to letters.

PROGRAMME

As full a programme should be staged as is possible, though obviously if a school has no pole vault facilities, for example, then it is difficult for them to find pole vaulters and impossible for them to stage the event on a return fixture. A typical inter-club programme is shown in the Appendix and can, of course, be adapted. Always keep in mind any restrictions that facilities or lack of them might impose upon your programme.

SCORING

Stick as closely as possible to conventional scoring patterns and avoid complicated types of scoring which mean that from the commencement of the meeting to about three-quarters of an hour after the final event nobody has any idea what the relative positions of the schools taking part is! Conventional scoring patterns are:

Dual meeting
Individual events   5 3 2 1
Relays   5 2
Triangular meeting
Individual events   7 5 4 3 2 1
Relays   10 7 3
Six-a-side school meeting
Individual events   12 10 8 6 5 4 (A)   8 6 4 3 2 1 (B)*
Relays   12 10 8 6 5 4

*in six-a-side matches, first and second string races will be required for events up to 1500 metres. In jumps and throws all competitors compete together with the first scoring athlete automatically scoring A points.

The important factor in such meetings is to ensure that every competitor (except where heats are involved) scores for his school.

OFFICIALS

More so than on sports days, outside officials can be used for the inter-school fixture, where the judicious placement of unbiased judgement can be useful. It is important to have experienced officials as: starter, referees and chief timekeeper. All that applies in the sports day section also applies here (see *Organising a sports day*).

In junior fixtures, senior pupils can be used to assist members of staff in officiating. A list of qualified officials can be obtained from County or Provincial associations or, as a second resort, from the area or national organisation (See Appendix B).

ORGANISATION

Make sure that your opponents have every piece of information they require well in advance. They need to know:

(1) Timetable of events
(2) Scoring system
(3) Time of starting
(4) Numbers alloted to their school
(5) Exact dates of age groupings
(6) Any restrictions on number of events per participants
(7) Number and types of officials they have to supply
(8) Refreshment information
(9) Directions to the venue

MEETING ORGANISATION

Much of this is included in the section *Organising a sports day*. Remember that you will be judged by your organisation of the meeting. Make the visiting school(s) welcome. It should not be difficult to ask the Parent-Teacher Association or parents of the competing athletes to organise refreshments after the meeting and most headmasters/ mistresses will agree to the cost being met out of school funds. Send details of the meeting to the local Press (and local radio if there is one). At the least they will send a photographer and you can send in a short report on the match, with results.

POST-MEETING WORK

Send a full set of results to the other school(s) with a short note thanking them for the fixture. Write also to outside officials who have assisted (it is a usual practice to offer the starter his 'ammunition money') and to parents who helped with refreshments. If the groundsman has been particularly helpful, a small gratuity would not go amiss.

DEALING WITH YOUR OWN TEAM

(1) Pick your team at least a week in advance *with reserves*. Make it clear to the latter that you expect them at the meeting with their gear

(2) If you have school colours make sure that every member of your team has them – especially newcomers. Check also that they all have numbers

(3) If you are deeply involved in the organisation of the meeting, try to get another member of staff to act as team manager

(4) For home fixtures have a team meeting the day before the match

(5) Get the captain to check for absentees a few days before the fixture and also on the day of the meeting so that reserves can be standing by

(6) In picking the team, resist the temptation to 'flog' a star athlete to death. Use him or her for maximum benefit, which may not necessarily be in their best event

(7) Ensure that they all do their best to make the visiting team(s) welcome

(8) Give them a definite time to report for the fixture

(9) Make it clear that you want them to stay for refreshments afterwards – never very difficult!

... AND AT AWAY FIXTURES

(1) Try to ensure that the team travels together. If a coach is to be hired then go to a reputable firm, ask him how long the journey

should take, and add one hour to ensure adequate warming-up time for the athletes in the early events and to allow for unexpected traffic hold-ups

(2) Make sure that any equipment (fibre-glass poles etc.) is ready for when the coach arrives. If travelling by train or, even worse, the underground, work out beforehand how such equipment is to be transported

(3) Ensure that you have all the information listed under *Organisation*

(4) Find out if any of the team suffers from coach/car sickness

(5) Try to take one member of staff with you to assist with the team

(6) Allow time for one social stop on the way back if the trip is above 20 miles

LEAGUE ATHLETICS

It is only a matter of time before some form of *local* school athletics league is formed and this may well be a development of the seventies. The organisation of league athletics is dealt with in the *Club Athletics* section but the obvious organisation to set up and run a local schools athletics league would be the District or, in more rural areas, the County Schools Association.

The reasons in favour of schools league athletics are much the same as for club league athletics. They give a purpose to having schools athletics competitions and certainly the role of the second string pole-vaulter, for example, who is just taking up the event is much enhanced; they give incentive both to the athletes and the schools and, by insisting on a full programme of events, the organisers are doing their tiny bit towards the improvement of the Cinderella field events in Britain.

Much the same applies to the possibility of a National Inter-Schools Cup competition as visualised for clubs in Britain for 1973. Run locally at first, then regionalised with a final meeting at one of Britain's major stadia such a competition – with one athlete per event which would cut down travelling costs and give the smaller schools a bigger opportunity – is certainly one that the English Schools Athletics Association, already slightly hamstrung by tradition and limited in its impact on schools athletics as a whole, could well consider.

3

Cross-country running and race walking

Cross-country running compared with the major winter team games is very much a minor sport in any school but nevertheless it has a very definite place and there are English Schools Cross-Country Championships for both boys and girls with the concommitant District and County Schools meetings.

The best way to find the cross-country runners is to run inter-form 'mob' matches on a games afternoon. A 'mob' match is, as the name implies, for a large number of runners and the essential factor is that as large a number of runners as possible should score, with the form with the *lowest* number of points being the winner. In all cross-country and road races the winner scores one point, the tenth runner ten points and so on. The course for such a race will vary – the secondary school in the London Borough of Islington for instance will have problems – and in some other urban areas the course will be on the road, where, perhaps, the 'mob' element will have to be lessened. Schools with their own playing fields or in the country will have little problem. Where some road or pavement is included, the normal precautions should be taken. From such races the better cross-country runners – and your track distance stars – will emerge. The first ones to discard are those already representing the school at team games, for they will not have the time to undertake even the minimum amount of training required to be an adequate cross-country runner. If it is not possible to organise regular cross-country matches then you should shunt the better runners along to the nearest athletic club which will, if it has nothing else, have a cross-country/road-running tradition and a wealth of fixtures.

FIXTURES

You will find that not many schools undertake regular cross-country fixtures and you should go about obtaining those that you can in much the same way as indicated in the previous section on inter-school track and field fixtures. Find out if there is a local cross-country league. Such leagues abound in Britain and there are often sections for all age groups for boys and girls. Local athletic clubs will also be glad to give you a fixture – the names and addresses of the immediate athletic clubs can be obtained from the County Association. You might also be able to obtain from them details of any junior, youth or girls road races in your area. Cross-country and road-running competition is, unless it is a very unusual area, not difficult to come by.

In addition to inter-school fixtures there are also the normal District and County or Provincial Cross-Country Championships. There are also the County and Area Men's and Women's Championships.

Competition should be obtained for as many as require it. Once a cross-country course is laid out and the officials obtained then the organisation and course may as well be used by the maximum number of people.

TYPES OF COURSE

Lay-out, types of course, officials are all dealt with in the cross-country section of *Club Athletics*. However the lengths of courses are important. The operative age date-time for cross-country for the English Schools Athletic Association is midnight, 1–2 September.

Boys
Junior (under 15)	not longer than 3 miles
Intermediate (15 and under 17)	not longer than 4 miles
Senior (17 and under 19)	not longer than 5 miles

Girls
Junior (under 15)	not longer than $1\frac{1}{2}$ miles
Intermediate (15 and under 17)	not shorter than $1\frac{1}{2}$ miles and not longer than 2 miles
Senior (17 and under 19)	not shorter than 2 miles and not longer than $2\frac{1}{2}$ miles

These distances should be taken as a guide and it may be a decided advantage to vary the length of match courses and to have some races over longer distances. Undoubtedly during the seventies the above distances will get longer.

Courses must always be clearly marked out and adequately marshalled.

FIXTURE DATES

Avoid matches in close proximity to major fixtures. Also avoid matches in mid-week during mock O and A Level exams and the mock CSE and any school exams generally. Saturday fixtures can be continued, adding some light relief to what is often a difficult time for school athletes.

CORRESPONDENCE

Write well in advance (during the summer and early autumn terms if possible); suggest a date and, if a new opponent, age groups and distances – if on your home course. Keep a copy of all correspondence and be prompt in writing and replying to letters.

ORGANISATION

Make sure that your opponents have every piece of information they require well in advance. They need to know:

(1) Commencement time of each race
(2) Numbers allotted to their school
(3) Exact dates of age groupings
(4) Numbers of officials you require from them
(5) Details of the course – if it includes road, pathway, plough, obstacles and *the type of footwear recommended*
(6) Refreshment information
(7) Directions to the venue

MEETING ORGANISATION

As with a track meeting you and your school will be judged on the organisation. Make the visiting school(s) welcome. It should not be difficult to ask the PTA or parents of the competing athletes to organise refreshments after the match – a hot drink is essential. Make sure that hot showers or a bath is available.

DEALING WITH YOUR OWN TEAM

(1) Pick your teams well in advance with reserves. Make it clear to the latter that you expect them to attend and there is really no reason why, with the agreement of the visitors, they cannot run not to score

(2) If you have school colours, make sure that every member of your team has them, especially the newcomers. Normal athletics vests are usually inadequate in winter conditions and the wearing of a long-sleeved football or hockey jersey underneath the vest is highly recommended. Discourage the wearing of gloves!

(3) If you are involved with the organisation try to get another member of staff to act as team manager

(4) For home fixtures have a team meeting the day before. Discuss tactics, the likely placing of the team, 'packing' and so on

(5) Get the captain to check on likely absentees

(6) Check on gear, especially running shoes taking into consideration the type of terrain to be run on

(7) Ensure that your team will do their best to make the visitors welcome

(8) A 'pep' talk always helps

. . . and at away fixtures

(1) Try to ensure that the team travels together. A coach is seldom required unless there is a large number of age groups so that a mini-bus or staff and parents' cars can be used – make sure that you will receive re-imbursement for this!

(2) Aim to arrive in time for a good warm-up

(3) Ensure that you have all the information listed under *organis-ation*

(4) Find out if any of the team suffers from car sickness

(5) Allow time for one social stop on the way back from the fixture if the journey is above 20 miles

POST-MEETING WORK

Gratuity for the groundsman if he has been helpful; write to parents who have helped with travelling or refreshments and write to the schools thanking them for the fixture.

CROSS-COUNTRY LEAGUES

As with track and field so with cross-country – perhaps even more so considering the numbers involved. The formation of a local cross-country league should present no problems and certainly would be a way of centralising and easing fixtures. Certainly cross-country leagues are immeasureably popular at club level and with junior girls. A great interest and enthusiasm for distance-running has been created in recent years. The obvious organisation to run such leagues would be the District Schools or County Schools Association.

RACE WALKING

Race walking is a fairly recent innovation in schools' athletics. The English Schools Athletics Association have a race walk in each category in the Boys section at their annual track championships (though each walk is held on a road circuit). These races are:

Junior boys	3000 metres
Intermediate boys	3000 metres
Senior boys	5000 metres

Race walking, be it on track or road, is a highly specialised section of the sport and those interested in fostering it at their school should contact the Race Walking Association who will readily forward information on clubs and coaches in the particular area together with details of competition.

4
Organising a sports day

What is the best sort of sports day? This is an important consideration which needs a good deal of thought. Often the organiser will arrive at a school where there is a definite tradition about its sports day – when it is held, what the events are, scoring and inter-house systems, presentation of prizes – all follow a pattern which has been the form, and much-loved form, for years. Even if he disagrees with the whole format the new physical education teacher would do well to leave it completely alone for the first year or so and even then introduce changes only gradually. Anyway, in his general thinking about athletics, sports day should only be a minor part.

There are varying ideas on the type of meeting a school sports day should be. The purists will insist on a completely bona-fide athletics meeting, probably following the national schools age group pattern but there are good arguments against this. This is the one day in the year when the whole school is concerned with the sport, albeit compulsorily, and also a day when a good number of parents could attend. The staff will be there in force. The worst thing possible would be to make it a boring day. You are selling the sport, so sell it well. Secondly, in many schools it is a social occasion as well as an athletics one so that anything too rigid and too spartan would not go down too well. Thirdly, it is a day when you want as many participants as possible. This is not to say that the whole afternoon should be spent with egg and spoon races and other such refinements but an equable blend of serious athletics and some light relief will make sports day something for everyone to look forward to rather than just another chore to attend. Recently one school introduced a minor form of the international television game 'It's a Knock-Out'; in a girls school why not a 'throwing a rolling pin' for parents and staff; in a boy's schools why not an 'obstacle race' for staff and parents ? Let the imagination go on these ancillary events.

The administration of a sports day can be divided into four components:

(1) Early preparation
(2) Late preparation
(3) The day of the meeting
(4) Post-meeting administration

EARLY PREPARATION

Preparation for sports day begins the previous autumn term with the deciding on the date. Many schools hold their sports days quite early in the summer term (we are assuming normality here and not the obsolete and slightly absurd publice school practice of staging athletics in the spring term) in order to find teams for the District Schools Championships or to get the day well out of the way. If tradition has not already firmly set the date then it would be well to consider staging the sports quite late in the summer term, after the main examinations. There are three good reasons for this:

(1) Examinations are over and students (and staff) can approach the day in a relaxed frame of mind
(2) Students will have had most of the term to practise (and in some cases train) at the events they have entered for
(3) For most boys or girls in the school sports day is the only serious type of meeting that they will compete in, and once it is over their interest quickly fades. By holding the event late in the summer term it will be something for them to aim at during the preceding weeks

On the opposite side there is the problem of organising teams for inter-school matches and district schools meetings but the organised athletics teacher will know most of his team anyway and a few judicious trials early in the term will sort out his juniors who will be the most unknown quantity. Other considerations when considering the date are to:

(1) Avoid the period of school external and internal examinations completely. Also avoid school camp dates, journeys and other main functions
(2) Choose two dates in case of extremely inclement weather causing a cancellation of the first

(3) Discuss the date with the headmaster and other main members of staff who hold functions during the summer term
(4) Avoid close proximity to school matches, county or national schools championships
(5) Make sure the track, if it has to be booked, is free for both your dates

Often the organiser has the choice between his own school ground or the local athletics track. The pros and cons here are almost equally divided and local fancies and dictates will be the final factor.

Programme content
Sports day itself should never be too long. A 2–2½ hour programme should suffice. Use the national schools age grouping dates and do not make the actual groups too numerous. Suggested age groupings are:

under 13 years		under 12 years
under 15 years	or	under 14 years
over 15 years		under 16 years
		over 16 years

Where possible, every athletic event should be catered for – *though this will mean that every final will not be held on sports day*, especially where field events are concerned. Choices can be made from:

Under 12 years	Under 13 years	Under 14/15 years	Over 15/16 years
100 metres*	100 metres*	100 metres*	100 metres*
200 metres*	200 metres*	200 metres*	200 metres*
		400 metres	400 metres*
	800 metres*	800 metres*	800 metres*
		1,500 metres	1,500 metres*
			3,000 metres Steeplechase
Hurdles*	Hurdles*	Hurdles*	Hurdles (2)*
	Race walk	Race walk	Race walk
High jump*	High jump*	High jump*	High jump*
Long jump*	Long jump*	Long jump*	Lond jump*
		Triple jump	Triple jump
	Pole vault	Pole vault	Pole vault
	Shot put*	Shot put*	Shot put*
		Discus throw*	Discus throw*
		Hammer throw	Hammer throw
		Javelin throw*	Javelin throw*
Relays*	Relays*	Relays*	Relays*
Ancillary events*			
*girls events			

Though a sprint relay is almost always essential the organiser can have further relays which could be 12 × 100 metres or 12 × 200 metres or medley relays or a continuous progressive relay (teams of 9, each running 50 metres) between Houses as a rousing finale to his meeting.

Timing of programme

Well organised school meetings are often the model of timing efficiency and we have all been to meetings where, relentlessly, year after year, as the first chime of 5 o'clock sounds, the headmaster presents the final trophy. Certainly this is to be preferred to the meeting that staggers on past 6 o'clock, running over an hour late. In many ways the organiser would be wise to keep his timing schedule to himself, announcing only the starting time of the meeting, but aiming to keep to the schedule that he has made out.

In most cases he will not be able to stage all his finals in one afternoon and he will need an extra afternoon or two to run off all track semi-finals and some field event finals. On the afternoon of sports day itself he should have a judicious mixture of all events, mixing the age groups together with the more light-hearted events. His timings should allow:

	Maximum	Minimum
Sprint events (100, 200, 400 metres)	5 minutes	2 minutes
Other track events	10/12 minutes	7/8 minutes
Hurdles events	10 minutes	10 minutes
Steeplechase and 3,000 metres	15 minutes	12 minutes
Relays	10 minutes	5 minutes
Race walk*	20/40 minutes	18/36 minutes
Pole vault	All afternoon	
High jump	60 minutes	45 minutes
Long jump	45 minutes	35 minutes
Triple jump	45 minutes	35 minutes
Shot put	45 minutes	35 minutes
Discus throw	60 minutes	45 minutes
Hammer throw	60 minutes	45 minutes
Javelin throw	75 minutes	60 minutes

*usually held away from the track on road or footpath

All of the above will depend upon the number of competitors, the standard of judging etc. and to attain the minimum schedule a some-what military approach to the day would certainly have to be organised. The timing of the more light-hearted events will depend absolutely upon their nature and the organiser should have one or two trial runs if he is unsure about the length of time that they will take.

The crucial events in timing and allotting the programme timetable are the hurdle events. If there is a 400 metres hurdles event, then this should always be the opening track event so that the hurdles may be placed on the track well before the commencement. If there is a series of hurdle events, then again it might be a good idea to start off with a whole series of them and to have a squad of pupils standing by ready to make the necessary adjustments to height and distance. Watch out for events in which athletes usually double-up, for example, 100, 200 and 400 metres, 100 metres and long jump, long and triple jump, and try to space them well apart in the programme. It saves time to group the various events under 13, under 15 and over 15 years 100 metres races so that they follow on from each other. The programme of events shown in the *Appendix* (which is for one age group only) is a good framework upon which a sports day timetable can be built.

Planning the preliminaries
The ways that athletes reach sports day itself are multifarious. The best system allows boys and girls, in the beginning, to enter as many events as they like in an attempt to attain standard points for their Houses. Once a boy has gained a standard then he can compete in the semi-final of that event unless numbers qualifying are small enough to enable him to go through to the final. At this stage the athlete must then choose his events on the assumption that he will qualify for the finals in all of them, according to the rules laid down governing the maximum number of events one athlete may compete in, for example, four events at least one of which must be a field event plus one relay. This is a restriction that should be enforced. These preliminaries can take up to two afternoons and these should be planned a sufficient time away from sports day itself so that if they are rained off they can be re-scheduled still some time before the final itself. The early standards in this case will have been run on normal games afternoons. Alternatively the organiser can run a series of straight heats with finalists emerging from a laid-down qualifying rule.

Inter-House competitions
In most schools these will be well ingrained but the organiser should make sure, through his planning, that one House does not reach sports day with an unassailable lead of points built up in the preliminaries. He can best avoid this by allocating a set number of points for the House obtaining the most number of standard points and so on. For example:

	Standard points	Sports Day points
Pitt House	356	50
Gladstone House	310	40
Lloyd George House	256	30
Churchill House	234	20

or the organiser may think it fairer to allocate points on a percentage basis with his 50 as maximum:

Pitt House	400	50
Gladstone House	300	37½
Lloyd George House	200	25
Churchill House	50	6

Invitations to officials

In most cases the staff will carry out all officiating duties and therefore invitations will be on an informal basis. Sometimes, however, outside officials are invited – usually qualified judges, starters or timekeepers – and invitations should go out to these well before the end of the previous year, for experience has shown that many are well booked up in advance.

All of the above decisions and actions should have been completed by the end of the autumn term. During the spring term additional items will have to be considered:

Entries

Normally taken at House meetings at the end of spring term. A full list of all events with the appropriate standard should be posted on the gymnasium and all House notice boards well before the date on which entries are taken.

Prize giving

What is the normal procedure? Does the headmaster or headmistress or Chief Education Officer or a governor or any of their wives or husbands carry out these duties? If not then a local celebrity in the sporting world may be a popular choice. An early invitation would be essential.

Dates

All dates for the preliminaries etc. should be finalised.

Officials

In most cases the staff of a school are well tried and trusted in officiating events. Mr Brown, the physics master, could well have been judging the javelin for fifteen successive sports days and, though he might not pass any judging award of a national association, there is a more than reasonable chance that the event will pass off smoothly. The new physical education teacher should tread warily on this ground and avoid any dramatic changes. Remember that you have to work with your colleagues for another thirty-nine weeks, four days! As well as taking such traditions into account the organiser should plan his judging teams with care. The following are minimum requirements and possible combinations:

Track events:	Referee	1		
	Judges	3		
	Timekeepers	3		
	Starter	1		
	Marksman	1	*Total*	9
Field events:	Referee	1		
Pole vault	Judges	3	(on all afternoon)	
High jump/shot put	Judges	3		
Discus/hammer/javelin	Judges	3		
Triple/long/jump	Judges	3	*Total*	13
Relay	Take-over Judges	6	(taken from field events)	

So the minimum requirement will be 22. With a larger staff, certainly a further team could be used to take the pressure off those judging the discus, hammer and javelin and, with still further staff, the amount of judging done by any one team can be reduced, thus giving them an opportunity to watch the rest of sports day. Race walking (if included) and any ancillary events should be covered by the track event team and a field event team.

With a smaller staff it may well be that senior pupils have to assist with the judging of field events.

The organiser now has to orientate his programme to allow for his team of officials and to make sure that they can cope with their duties comfortably. With the above combinations he must obviously avoid clashes of high jump and shot put and of discus, hammer and javelin but it must now be obvious that with three or four age groups a good number of field events must be held before sports day itself.

It may well be a good idea to call a brief meeting of the staff prior to the sports so that both the organiser and the officials can raise points – for him to put forward changes in the competition rules which may have occurred since the previous year and for the staff to raise any point which they are not clear on. *It would help a great deal if copies of the relevant rules could be photo-copied and pasted on to card and given to the judges* along with the field-event competition card.

An outline of each official's task is given below:

Referee (track and field) Often this is, by tradition, the headmaster, but unless he is an experienced official with full knowledge of the competition rules it may be a wise move to suggest to him or her well beforehand that he or she take the post of President of the Meeting so that he or she may carry out his social functions properly. The referees are the final arbiters of all decisions and consequently must have a fair knowledge of the competition rules, even for a school sports day. There is a temptation, therefore, for the physical education teacher to take this role, but it is one that he should resist, leaving himself with a roving commission all the afternoon. If the meeting is a fair-sized one have a referee for both track and field events.

Track judges The organiser and the referee should acquaint themselves beforehand with the method the judges are most familiar with in judging track events. This is not likely to be an approved AAA method and is more likely to be:

Referee	All six
Miss Jones	1 2 3
Miss Smith	2 3 4
Miss Green	4 5 6

With more judges further duplication can take place. The organiser or referee should avoid drastic action as in insisting that the judges 'take all six' for they are more likely in the ensuing confusion of a 100 metre race to get none at all! As a gradual process all judges assessing the places of all six competitors could begin with the long track events.

Timekeepers Try and have as many times taken as possible. There is a strong case for bringing in one or two qualified timekeepers from the local list of AAA/WAAA/Scottish/Irish timekeepers for not only will they be able to organise your school timekeepers to best advantage but they are capable of taking a large number of times themselves, especially in the longer events.

Starter   If there is a large number of events two starters can be used but it is rare to find two competent starters on a school staff. The starter is in absolute control of the start and his decisions appertaining to the starting of races is final.

Marksman/men   The duty here is to assist the starter by ensuring that the competitors are sited properly as per programme and/or lane draw and also in the correct position at the start i.e. fingers behind the line etc. This is especially helpful to the starter when staggered starts are being used. When all competitors are ready the marksman will indicate this to the starter.

Take-over judges   Not always the best performed duty at a school sports day. There should be at least two people per take-over zone and you should ensure that they are absolutely clear about the rules of the event, especially those that are recruited for the task at the last moment.

Pole vault judges   (1) to call out the competitors and mark the card; (2) and (3) to assist with measuring and raising the bar. This is a complicated and drawn-out event and the sooner the organiser can bring an experienced team together the better. It may well require the buying of a few pints at the end of each sports day but it will be well worth it!

High jump judges   (1) to call out the competitors and mark the card; (2) and (3) to assist with the measuring and raising of the bar and ensuring that the landing area is kept in safe condition.

(Together, high jump and pole vault judges, must know the count-back rule and how to apply it (see national rules for competition). Field event referees should carefully check both cards.)

Long and triple jump   (1) to call out the competitors mark the card and judge the legality of each jump; (2) and (3) to measure each jump and ensure adequate raking of the pit.

Shot put   (1) to call out the competitors, mark the card and judge the legality of each put; (2) and (3) to measure each put and supervise the return of the implements.

Hammer, discus and javelin (1) to call out the competitors, mark the card and judge the legality of each throw; (2) and (3) to measure each throw and supervise the return of the implements. Try to avoid the older members of staff judging these events as the implements are likely to fall anywhere within a wide area ensuring a fair amount of running about. If the necessary length of tape is available then each throw should be measured; if not then throws will have to be pegged (with the peg on the longest throw) and extra stewards will be required for this task.

Other officials In addition to the 'technical officials' there are other positions that must be filled for a sports day to run smoothly. These are:

(1) Announcer
(2) Competitors stewards
(3) Officials stewards
(4) Gate stewards (if a charge is being made)
(5) Programme stewards
(6) Enclosure stewards
(7) Clerk of the course
(8) Recorders

Announcer To many the success or failure of a meeting can depend on the success or failure of the announcer and the organiser should liaise closely with him to decide on the sort of presentation that is to be made. With a long meeting with complications, it may be a good idea to have two announcers, with contrasting voices, and allot tasks. Good announcers can usually be found in the drama department. Reference should be made to the appropriate club section dealing with announcing.

Competitors stewards The duties of the competitors stewards are to ensure that all competitors are ready for their event an alloted time before its commencement (for a school sports day 15 minutes should be adequate). For this purpose there should be an area designated as the competitors' marshalling area where the competitors can report to the stewards. Make it perfectly clear that Houses or forms or even individuals are responsible for ensuring that competitors are in the marshalling area at the appropriate time. Five minutes before the event the stewards should take the competitors en masse to the start or field event area. These duties can be adequately performed by senior pupils not involved in competing on the day.

Officials' stewards All officials should be allotted a number of stewards to carry out various tasks, e.g. raking the pit, transporting the implements back to throwing areas, taking the results from referees to the recorders and announcers. These tasks can be adequately carried out by pupils.

Gate stewards If some form of entrance is being paid, then gate stewards will be required. Senior pupils can easily fill this role but a member of staff should be in charge.

Programme stewards Ensure an adequate number of programmes and programme stewards. Pupils can again fulfil this function.

Enclosure stewards or VIP stewards or parents' stewards or guests' stewards. If people from outside the school are visiting the sports, then adequate provision should be made to have them received and seated somewhere where they can watch the sports in comparative comfort and comparative peace. If VIPs are visiting then the headmaster in his role of President of the Meeting should receive and entertain them.

Clerk of the course Often this duty is performed by the organiser or the physical education teacher or the groundsman. Whoever it is it is his duty to ensure that (i) all track markings are available and known and (ii) all equipment is available. This should be done in the morning prior to the sports. It may be necessary for him to sign for such equipment at the beginning of the day and to ensure that it is all returned at the end of the meeting. These duties will commence early in the morning and he should ensure that all is ready half an hour before the meeting is due to begin.

Recorders A combination of the arts and mathematics departments usually fulfils these roles very competently. They should be situated close to the announcer(s) so that results can be passed along easily and inter-house team scores can be frequently fed to the announcers. The organiser should try to ensure a simple method of recording to allow swiftness in communicating results and scores. All the sheets should be prepared well in advance and both recorders and announcers should not be subject to any inclement weather that might occur.

LATE PREPARATION (SUMMER TERM)

During the summer term the organiser will begin his administration for

COMPETITION		HIGH JUMP										
VENUE		POLE VAULT										
DATE	EVENT	LONG JUMP TRIPLE JUMP DISCUS, JAVELIN, WEIGHT, HAMMER	1ST TRIAL	2ND TRIAL	3RD TRIAL	BEST	PLACE	4TH TRIAL	5TH TRIAL	6TH TRIAL	FINAL BEST
NO.	NAME	CLUB—COUNTRY									

RESULT		FT.	INS.	METRES		STANDARDS	
1st							
2nd							
3rd					REFEREE		JUDGE
4th					JUDGE		JUDGE
5th					OBTAINABLE FROM		
6th					**AMATEUR ATHLETIC ASSOCIAT**		

Figure 2

sports day. He will have scrutinised the entries and as standards are achieved or heats are completed, so semi-finals and finals will be drawn. It is recommended that all 'drawing' of lanes etc. should be completed prior to the day. If, as in many schools, standards are 'run off' during normal games periods, then there is no problem but, if special after-noons are set aside for the running of heats, these should be drawn well in advance (and judiciously seeded) and posted on notice boards. The same will apply to semi-finals and finals.

Track and field event cards
These can be obtained in bulk from the Amateur Athletic Association.

Alternatively they can be typed out (see figure 2), photo-copied and pasted onto boards. There should be an adequate supply of both kinds. In the case of the track result cards there is a strong case for these being on thinnish paper so that the track referee can carbon two or more copies of the result – one for the recorders and one for the announcers. This will expedite the flow of the meeting considerably.

Other pre-day tasks that must be carried out by the organiser are:

Public address system
Go to a reputable firm and order this well in advance. Make sure that it is installed and ready for use at least $1\frac{1}{2}$ hours before the commencement time of the meeting.

Refreshments
Ensure that adequate refreshments are available – ice-cream vans etc. If teas are required for staff and VIPs and visitors contact the caterer well in advance.

Press
Make sure that the Press (and in some cases local radio) are made aware of the date and time of your sports day and get an understanding of what they require from you. In some cases they will send along a reporter and a cameraman; in other cases only the latter will attend for a brief time and the sports editor will then require a full set of results and perhaps a short report from you. In any case, give them all the assistance that you can and if more than one or two people are involved, supply a Press steward (a glamorous sixth former). If results are required then bribe or coerce the school administrative staff to type them out and have duplicating equipment ready.

Track liaison
Make sure that the groundsman of the track (even if it is your own school playing field) has a copy of the timetable of events well in advance and knows your requirements. This applies especially to those events which are outside the normal run of things.

Programme
If this is to be a printed affair then make sure that you have a date from the printer for final copy. Make sure that everyone's name is spelt correctly. Check the proof yourself. If the programme is being

duplicated, make sure that the office staff have considerable time to prepare it.

Required items
Make a check-list of all required items. A comprehensive check-list is shown in the *Appendix* though not all the items shown there will be required for a school sports day. In many cases, where the track is hired, items will already be provided but they should still be checked out. Check each item with a tick as it is confirmed.

Outside officials
If outside officials are being invited make sure that they receive full information, including confirmation that they are still required, directions to the school/track etc. between two and three weeks in advance. This information should also include number of judges available for various events (together with an appraisal of their experience), number of timekeepers (and watches!) available. This enables them to think out beforehand how they will organise their officiating.

Presentation of the meeting
During this time the organiser should give some thought to the format his meeting will take and the sort of presentation he wants his announcers to give. The fact that it is a school sports day should not mean that little thought should be given to this aspect. To revert to a previous theme: sports day should not be a chore for all concerned. Link up with the headmaster about presentations. Half an hour of cup and certificate presenting at the end of the day is never very popular and usually ends with the headmaster, the organiser, the presenter of the trophies, the winners and a few hangers on all huddled together in a waste-land of a sports field going through the motions. All will depend on the number of trophies available but it is a good idea, if there are a good few, to keep trophy presentations going throughout the afternoon without any formal ceremonies, apart from the final inter-House or *victor-ludorum* at the end. Another alternative is to slot into the programme special times for presentations – about five minutes for an allotted number.

Each school will have its own different slant to sports day. For some it is the individual battles in each event that predominate; for others the inter-House battles are the main feature. Whatever it is make sure that the announcer(s) keep the interest and pace going. Especially important is slickness in announcing results, and if presentations are going on all afternoon, these should be tied in with the announcing of the result. All in all, the points made on announcing and presentation in the club section apply equally well to a school sports day but are so much easier in that the announcer(s) will know all the competitors. Remember too that parents will likely be watching, so any outstanding performers that the school has should be pointed out.

Play music both before and after the meeting.

THE DAY OF THE MEETING

Arrive early in the day.

(1) Inspect the track or field with the clerk of the course. Note any deficiencies and have them rectified immediately

(2) Have two tried and trusted senior pupils as your personal assistants

(3) Check if any members of staff are absent

(4) Check if any finalists are absent. Have you a reserve list?

(5) Re-check your list of required items and make sure that any deficiencies previously noted have been rectified

(6) Check with all members of staff to make sure they are happy

(7) Check with the headmaster to make sure that all his arrangements are going smoothly

(8) Make sure that any announcements that have to be made to the whole school (and there are usually quite a lot) are with the headmaster so that he can make them at morning assembly

(9) Check the local weather forecast

(10) Check out the refreshment arrangements, especially with regard to the timing of staff and officials' refreshments. It is unwise to try and allow for the judges to take their refreshments during the meeting itself but it must be certain that there will be some left by the end of the meeting! Cups of tea could, however, be taken out onto the track during the afternoon

(11) Double-check all field event equipment

(12) Make sure that the public address system, when it arrives, is placed in the most advantageous position and tested. Try to ensure that a technician from the firm remains with the equipment during the meeting

(13) Ensure a prompt start to the first events

(14) Keep in touch with all events throughout the afternoon. Keep

35

on the move looking out for problems so that they can be dealt with quickly

(15) Begin preparations for the final ceremonies about twenty minutes before the commencement of the last event

Post-meeting work (on the day)

(1) Ensure that all necessary payments have been made
(2) Give the groundsman a gratuity commensurate with the work he has done and the support he has given you
(3) Ensure that all monies (gate receipts or programme sales) has been collected
(4) Make sure that all officials' badges have been collected
(5) Make sure that a full set of results is available for you
(6) Make sure that all spare trophies have been collected
(7) Check that all field-event equipment has been safely returned
(8) Thank all the officials you can find
(9) Collect all lost property

POST-MEETING WORK (AFTER THE DAY)

(1) Re-visit the track or field the next morning with a class of boys to assist with the clearing up and the removal of any school equipment
(2) Make sure that you thank anyone whom you did not see immediately after the end of the meeting
(3) Set in motion the engraving of trophies
(4) Write and thank anyone from outside the school who assisted
(5) Make sure that all accounts are paid
(6) Find out, tactfully, whether the headmaster wrote to the visiting VIPs
(7) Begin next year's file with:
    (a) A full set of this year's results
    (b) A copy of the programme *with the new records clearly entered*
    (c) Copies of all the results sheets
    (d) Lists of names and addresses of all outside officials who helped
    (e) Names and addresses of suppliers of public address system, of the caterers, printers etc
    (f) Suggestions based on the experience gained from this year's sports

(g) All the necessary information to help a newcomer run the event – who knows where you will be in twelve months time?

A blend of athleticism, excitement, mass identification (with Houses or individuals), and even show-biz can make sports days quite memorable affairs which can slot comfortably into the physical education and athletics programme of schools of every dimension. They can also form the framework round which to build any track and field meetings the school might stage.

5

Incentive schemes

Physical education teachers should be constantly thinking about how they can add a new dimension to sport and recreation in their school, how they can increase interest and event participation. Even the most successful sports need new injections of ideas and life from time to time to avoid any suggestion of staleness or complacency. New stimulus and new incentives can increase ambition, set new targets for the athletes.

By far the biggest incentive scheme yet devised in track and field athletics has been the Amateur Athletic Association's Five-Star Award Scheme which is involving hundreds of thousands of youngsters each year in a form of athletic competition.

Based on the decathlon type of competition each youngster performs, with unlimited numbers of attempts in either practice or competition, against scoring tables in any three chosen events, including one field and one track event. From his total points score for three events he obtains an appropriate certificate and can purchase a badge for his particular age group. Overall standards required to obtain the lower grade awards are not high and the whole scheme has added a purpose to what was often an aimless athletics afternoon on a games day. As an introduction to the competitive side of the sport it is ideal.

On the 1972 Scoring Tables a 13-year-old might achieve:
    100 metres in 14.6 secs.
    high jump—4 ft. (1 metre 22 cm)
    long jump—12 ft. 10 in. (3 metres 91 cm)
and obtain a Three-Star Award.

For the school athletics club that consistently hits a reasonable standard, competitive tours are often an excellent spur to athletes hoping to make the school team. Such tours can either be in Britain or abroad and two or three matches can be arranged to cover a period of two or three or more days. The best approach is to contact the appropriate County or Area Schools Association (addresses can be obtained from the appropriate national association or handbook) and ask for the contacts at schools in their area of similar standing and enthusiasm. Such visits can be on a reciprocal basis or a single tour of the area in question by your school. For such visits abroad the British Amateur Athletic Board will put you in touch with the appropriate national association who will, in turn, put you in touch with the appropriate schools association.

Some schools organise trips to major meetings (international matches, national schools championships etc.). Some visit regularly the two major stadia at Crystal Palace or Meadowbank in Edinburgh or in Ireland at the John F. Kennedy Stadium in Dublin. Certainly for youngsters keen on athletics the chance to see some of the top competitors in action and to take in the atmosphere of a big international meeting is one that they will savour for some time. Even in the winter there are regular top meetings on the indoor track at RAF Cosford, near Wolverhampton and indoor meetings have also begun at the Bell Sports Centre at Perth in Scotland. One of the tendencies of the seventies will be to take more important meetings to choice venues around the country and this will give greater opportunity for schools athletes to see internationals in action. For the more ambitious, trips to major international meetings such as the European Championships and Olympic Games have become a regular occurrence.

Visits by local athletics personalities and coaches (though the term is relative!), arranging for youngsters to assist with stewarding at local trophy and other meetings, entering the better athletes for bigger grade meetings can all act as incentives. The vital thing is to keep the momentum going.

Senior Men			European Junior Men			Junior Men/Senior Schools		
18 yrs of age on day of competition			Under 19 years of age			Operative date for 1973:-		
			On 1st Jan in year of competition			After September 1st 1954		
Operative year for 1973 : 1955			Operative year for 1973:- 1954			Before September 2nd 1956		

74	75	76	77	78	79	74	75	76	77	78	79	74	75	76	77	78	7
56	57	58	59	60	61	55	56	57	58	59	60	55 / 57	56 / 58	57 / 59	58 / 60	59 / 61	60 /

110 metres			110 metres			110 metres		
3'6" / 106·7cm	10 flights		3'6" / 106·7cm	10 flights		3'3" / 99·00cm	10 flights	
Distance to first hurdle	Distance between hurdles	Last hurdle to finish	Distance to first hurdle	Distance between hurdles	Last hurdle to finish	Distance to first hurdle	Distance between hurdles	Last hurdle to finish
13·72 m	9·14 m	14·02 m	13·72 m	9·14 m	14·02 m	13·72m	9·14m	14·02m

200 metres						200 metres		
2'6" / 76cm	10 flights					2'6" / 76cm	10 flights	
Distance to first hurdle	Distance between hurdles	Last hurdle to finish				Distance to first hurdle	Distance between hurdles	Last hurdle to finish
18·29m	18·29m	17·10m				18·29m	18·29m	17·10m

400 metres			400 metres			400 metres		
3'0" / 91·4cm	10 flights		3'0" / 91·4cm	10 flights		3'0" / 91·4cm	10 flights	
Distance to first hurdle	Distance between hurdles	Last hurdle to finish	Distance to first hurdle	Distance between hurdles	Last hurdle to finish	Distance to first hurdle	Distance between hurdles	Last hurdle to finish
45m	35m	40m	45m	35m	40m	45m	35m	40m

7·257Kg (16lbs)			7·257Kg (16lbs)			6·25Kg (13lbs 8ozs)		
2Kg (4lbs 6·5ozs)			2Kg (4lbs 6·5ozs)			1·75Kg (3lbs 13·75ozs)		
7·257Kg (16lbs)			7·257Kg (16lbs)			6·25Kg (13lbs 8ozs)		
800gr (1lb 12·218ozs)			800gr (1lb 12·218ozs)			800gr (1lb 12·218ozs)		
3,000 metres			2,000 metres			2,000 metres		
28 hurdles		3'0"	28 hurdles		3'0"	17 hurdles		3'0"
7 water jumps		91·4cm	7 water jumps		91·4cm	4 water jumps		91·4cm

Youths/Intermediate Schools					Boys/Junior Schools							
Operative dates for 1973:-					Operative dates for 1973:-							. AGE GROUPS
After September 1st 1956					After September 1st 1958							
Before September 2nd 1958					Before September 2nd 1960							
75	76	77	78	79	74	75	76	77	78	79		
58	59	60	61	62	59	60	61	62	63	64		
9 / 60	61	62	63	64	61	62	63	64	65	66		

100 metres			80 metres			HURDLES
'0" / 91·45cm	10 flights		2'9" / 83·8cm	8 flights		
tance to t hurdle	Distance between hurdles	Last hurdle to finish	Distance to first hurdle	Distance between hurdles	Last hurdle to finish	
13m	8·5m	10·5m	12m	8m	12m	
						LOW HURDLES
						INTER-MEDIATE HURDLES
5Kg (11lbs)			4Kg (8lb 13ozs)			SHOT PUT
1·5Kg (3lb 4·75oz)			1·25Kg (2lb 12 ozs)			DISCUS THROW
5Kg (11lbs)			4Kg (8lb 13ozs)			HAMMER THROW
700gr (1 lb 8·691ozs)			600gr (1lb 5·163ozs)			JAVELIN THROW
1,500 metres						STEEPLE-CHASE

Notes

(1) Under AAA Laws certain athletes may compete in certain senior events before 18 (see AAA Rules for Competition)

(2) Irish Schools operative date is August 1st

(3) In Junior Men/Senior Schools section an athlete has an additional year in schools competition so that for 1973 operative dates are:
After September 1st.1953
Before September 2nd 1956.
and so on.

(4) In Boys/Junior Schools section and Junior Girls section note that only top operative date applies

Cross-country

(1) For schools operative age dates as for track and field

(2) Cross-country for Boys confined to competitors who have reached their 14th but not 16th birthdays on September 1st prior to competition

(3) For Youths the age dates are 16 and 18 as per above

(4) For Juniors the age dates are 18 and 20 as per above

(5) For women the operative date is midnight September 1/2 preceding the competition

Girls	11 and under 12
Juniors	12 and under 14
Inter	14 and under 16
Senior	16 and over

Road running

(1) Operative age dates:-
Races between 1/4 & 31/8 : 1/4
Races between 1/9 & 31/3 : 1/9

Boys	14 & 15 years of age
Youths	16 & 17 years of age
Juniors	18 & 19 years of age

(2) For women as cross-country

Race walking

(1) As per track and field

(2) Women as per track and field

Senior Women						European Junior Women						Senior Girls Schools					
15 yrs and over						Under 18 years of age on						Operative date for 1973:-					
On Sept. 1/2 (midnight)						1st Jan. in year of competition						After September 1st 1954					
Operative year for 1973:- 1958						Operative year for 1973:- 1955						Before September 2nd 1956					
74	75	76	77	78	79	74	75	76	77	78	79	74	75	76	77	78	79
59	60	61	62	63	64	56	57	58	59	60	61	55/57	56/58	57/59	58/60	59/61	60/

100 metres			100 metres			100 metres		
2'9" / 83·8cm	10 flights		2'9" / 83·8cm	10 flights		2'9" / 83·8cm	10 flights	
Distance to first hurdle	Distance between hurdles	Last hurdle to finish	Distance to first hurdle	Distance between hurdles	Last hurdle to finish	Distance to first hurdle	Distance between hurdles	Last hurdle to finish
13m	8·5m	10·5m	13m	8·5m	10·5m	13m	8·5m	10·5m

200 metres		
2'6" / 76cm	10 flights	
Distance to first hurdle	Distance between hurdles	Last hurdle to finish
16m	19m	13m

Senior Women	European Junior Women	Senior Girls Schools
4Kg (8lb 13oz)	4Kg (8lb 13 ozs)	4Kg (8lb 13 ozs)
1Kg (2lb 3·25oz)	1Kg (2lb 3·25ozs)	1Kg (2lb 3·25ozs)
600gr (1lb 5·163ozs)	600gr (lb 5·163ozs)	600gr (1lb 5·163ozs)

Intermediate Women/ Intermediate Schools	Junior Women/Junior Schools	
Operative date for 1973:-	Operative dates for 1973:-	
After September 1st 1956	After September 1st : 1958	
Before September 2nd 1958	Before September 2nd :- 1962	**AGE GROUPS**

4	75	76	77	78	79	74	75	76	77	78	79
58	59	60	61	62		59	60	61	62	63	64
59	60	61	62	63	64	63	64	65	66	67	68

80 metres			75 metres			
2'6" / 76cm	8 flights		2'6" / 76cm	8 flights		**HURDLES**
tance to t hurdle	Distance between hurdles	Last hurdle to finish	Distance to first flight	Distance between hurdles	Last hurdle to finish	
12m	8m	12m	11·5m	7·5m	11m	

		LOW HURDLES
		INTERMEDIATE HURDLES
4Kg (8lb 13 ozs)	3·25Kg (7lb 2·5 ozs)	**SHOT PUT**
1Kg (2lb 3·25ozs)	1Kg (2lb 3·25ozs)	**DISCUS THROW**
		HAMMER THROW
600gr (1lb 5·163ozs)	600gr (1lb 5·163ozs)	**JAVELIN THROW**
		STEEPLE CHASE

Notes

(1) Under AAA Laws certain athletes may compete in certain senior events before 18 (see AAA Rules for Competition)

(2) Irish Schools operative date is August 1st

(3) In Junior Men/Senior Schools section an athlete has an additional year in schools competition so that for 1973 operative dates are:
After September 1st.1953
Before September 2nd 1956
and so on.

(4) In Boys/Junior Schools section and Junior Girls section note that only top operative date applies

Cross-country

(1) For schools operative age dates as for track and field

(2) Cross-country for Boys confined to competitors who have reached their 14th but not 16th birthdays on September 1st prior to competition

(3) For Youths the age dates are 16 and 18 as per above

(4) For Juniors the age dates are 18 and 20 as per above

(5) For women the operative date is midnight September 1/2 preceding the competition

Girls	11 and under 12
Juniors	12 and under 14
Inter	14 and under 16
Senior	16 and over

Road running

(1) Operative age dates:-
Races between 1/4 & 31/8 : 1/4
Races between 1/9 & 31/3 : 1/9

Boys	14 & 15 years of age
Youths	16 & 17 years of age
Juniors	18 & 19 years of age

(2) For women as cross-country

Race walking

(1) As per track and field

(2) Women as per track and field

43

Club Athletics

6

General Management

The organisation of athletics in Britain is, for historical reasons, an administrative complexity. Though the beginning of the seventies has seen some attempt being made to rationalise a situation which exemplifies, more than any other sport, Parkinson's Law, many prejudices and concepts are so deeply felt and sincerely held that the progress towards a united British Federation may well be a long one.

In a nutshell, the administration of athletics could be said to be diamond-shaped with an integrated (in most cases) club at the bottom branching out into many organisations and committees at various levels, finally coming together again in one body at the top, the British Amateur Athletic Board which deals with international commitments and directs the running of the United Kingdom coaching scheme. The process at present under way, albeit slowly, is to form a British Federation composed of the various area associations in England together with the associations in Northern Ireland, Scotland and Wales which will effectively render obsolete the Amateur Athletic Association and the Women's Amateur Athletic Association who are, at the present time, responsible for the administration of men's and women's athletics in England respectively.

In order of ascendancy from the club itself are the following organisations in England and Wales:

COUNTY ASSOCIATIONS

These exist in most counties in England and Wales, though in some cases counties have combined. Most counties have separate men's and women's associations though again some have come together to form one organisation. In the area covered by the Northern Counties Athletic Association most of the work, with the exception of county championships, is carried out by district committees which do not necessarily follow any county boundary but may take up one or more counties or part of a county. Thus, in the north of England a men's county association does little more than run a county championship meeting each year. Unless changes are made along with the political and physical changes due in 1974 then the effectiveness of the present associations will decrease even further.

AREA ASSOCIATIONS

In any re-organisation of athletics in Britain these organisations look like remaining more or less in their present form. In England there are Southern, Midland and Northern Associations for both men and women and at present the Welsh AAA is represented both on the British Amateur Athletic Board and the Amateur Athletic Association.

In addition the Southern AAA has two off-shoot sub-areas, the Eastern Counties and the South-Western Counties AAA, who exist for administrative purposes.

NATIONAL ASSOCIATIONS

The Amateur Athletic Association is the oldest association in the world. It governs men's athletics in England and Wales at the present time. It has a full-time Administrative Officer and some secretarial staff.

The Women's Amateur Athletic Association governs women's athletics in England and Wales.

SCOTLAND

Scotland has a number of district associations and a few county associations. The district associations are closely linked with the Scottish Amateur Athletics Association which governs men's athletics in that country.

An identical pattern exists for women's athletics under the Scottish WAAA.

NORTHERN IRELAND

Most clubs in Northern Ireland are represented direct to the Northern Ireland AAA and/or the Northern Ireland WAAA.

45

BRITISH AMATEUR ATHLETIC BOARD

The British Amateur Athletic Board came into being in 1932 at the International Amateur Athletics Federation's insistence that all the various associations in Britain should be represented by one organisation to deal with international affairs. Since then it has dealt mainly with the organisation of international matches, both at home and abroad, international selections for matches and for European and Olympic teams (for Commonwealth Games this selection is undertaken by the various appropriate associations in Britain). In 1972 the BAAB took over the organisation and direction of coaching in Britain under the United Kingdom coaching scheme.

IRELAND

If the organisation of athletics in Britain may be looked upon as complex then in Ireland it could be considered an administrative perplexity. It is hardly surprising that Irish athletics has for most of its history been steeped in political controversy. In the Republic of Ireland there are two associations, one of which, the Bord Luthchleas Na h'Eireann (BLE) is recognised by the IAAF. The second is the National Athletics and Cycling Association (NACA) which is an off-shoot of the highly political Gaelic Athletic Association and is dedicated to one governing body for the whole of the thirty-two counties in Ireland. Athletes organised under the latter organisation are prohibited from taking part in BLE and IAAF events.

In Northern Ireland there are three organisations. Two of them, the Northern Ireland AAA and the Northern Ireland WAAA are affiliated to the British Amateur Athletic Board but the third is an independent, outlawed (by the IAAF) body called the Ulster Sports Council also dedicated to one governing body for the thirty-two counties in Ireland.

In certain sports, rugby and hockey being prime examples, there is one association for the whole of the country and various attempts have been made over the years to bring the various belligerent parties together without much success. Certainly any future discussions will rest upon some improvement in the volatile political situation and be preceded by twelve months of general amnesty.

INTERNATIONAL AMATEUR ATHLETIC FEDERATION

Founded in 1912 it is composed of 'duly elected national governing

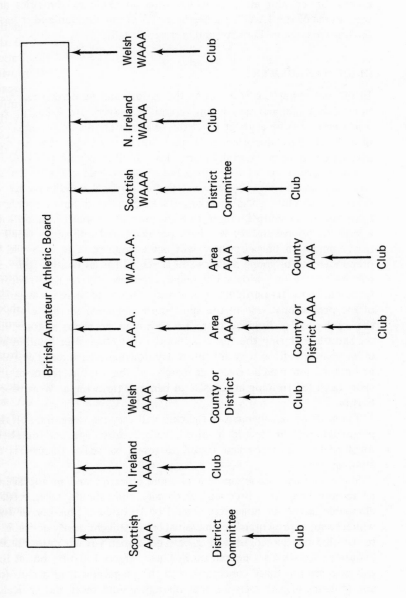

Figure 3

bodies for amateur athletics which agree to abide by the rules and regulations of the IAAF'. Its headquarters are in London and it has a full-time Executive Director and secretarial staff.

CLUB MANAGEMENT

In the end, though, it is not upon the various and numerous organisations that a national association should be judged. Its strengths and weaknesses will be a direct reflection of the strengths and weaknesses of its single most important unit: the club. It is a lesson that national associations have not yet fully learnt, least of all in Britain and Ireland.

The management of three hundred or so athletic clubs in Britain will vary enormously, because social and physical conditions are so diverse. The club official in Cornwall faces quite different problems from the one in south London; in turn, the club in south London with a long, traditional history will have problems and difficulties which a newly organised one elsewhere will not encounter. The club with a preponderence of young athletes still at school has an entirely different outlook to the one with a big senior cross-country or road-running tradition. In the far north of England and in Scotland there is a wariness of the professional side of the sport quite unknown in the south; in the south-west of England there are enormous problems in travelling on Saturdays during the summer months that officials in London are often unaware of. So it is difficult to lay down any hard and fast rules of organisation which cover adequately all the various facets of the sport from fell running at Eskdale to hammer throwing at Wormwood Scrubs.

The style of management of the club will vary too depending on the personality of the people involved, club history, age and numbers involved but the important factor, to revert to earlier themes, is to attain success.

Success means the attainment of some objective and in appraising or re-appraising the direction which any club should take, certain attainable targets or objectives should be laid down, plus one or two which seem, at present, to be unattainable but still eminently desirable – to use that oft quoted Browning passage 'a man's reach must exceed his grasp else what's a heaven for?' These targets will vary but at the end of a season, those concerned with the management of a club (or any athletics organisation for that matter) should meet and critically assess the club's performance, its strengths and its weaknesses, the triumphs and failures and then make appropriate plans for the future in the light of what happened. Is there too big an imbalance between track and field? Does the cross-country team have enough reserve strength to cope with injury and illness? Were home fixtures well organised? Were there enough funds for travelling? How about the social side this year? Has the junior and youth policy worked? Did the women's section have enough fixtures? And, most importantly, is the club's management adequate or is the burden falling too much on one or two people?

Critical self-assessment is difficult for any group of people to carry out especially in a sport where, because of the honorary nature of the work, criticism is taken very personally. To quote one well known club official writing to *Athletics Weekly* early in 1972: 'Anybody who criticised my organisation or work on the track would receive an immediate invitation to take the job over and show me how to do it . . .' But so many clubs have suffered because no one had the heart to tell one of the key officials, who has probably been there for fifteen years or more, that he has been doing too much, that the volume of work had increased so much that it was impossible for one to do it adequately any more. So the club and the athletes suffer. The rather macabre test which every official should put to himself is: if I died tomorrow would this club continue in exactly the same way as it does now? The answer should be, yes.

For a club to thrive it must be strong in every section from seniors to the youngest members, both men and women. Some clubs, many of them famous with long traditions of success, have forgotten this and are falling by the wayside in the increasingly competitive situation in which clubs are today finding themselves. This is a very special situation for the club hamstrung with a large general committee over-weighted with men or women who have completely lost contact with the sport and fail to appreciate that the social context in which athletics takes place has changed completely since 1935. Tragically, these men and women play no active administrative role in the running of the club and totally inhibit the small band of workers struggling to take the club into the second half of the twentieth century. Even more tragically this attitude has no equation with old age and the call for 'young men' to enter the sport's administration does not necessarily mean a sudden rush of new ideas and positive thinking. On the other hand if the active athletes are determined enough – and willing enough to take on organisational work – then changes can be made which will give the club new impetus and life, as clearly shown by the Polytechnic Harriers in 1971 and 1972 after two or three years of near disaster in the National League. *But people must be willing to undertake the work of pushing the club forward.*

South London Harriers is another famous name in athletics. Founded in 1871, its halcyon years came just after the war and during the fifties when its name was synonymous with its most famous athlete, Gordon Pirie. Yet in its centenary year it was languishing in Division 4 of the Southern League and being kept alive mainly by the efforts of one man, Bill Thomas, who has been its secretary since 1947. What has caused its lean spell? Three main reasons, two of vital importance: failure to maintain a steady flow of recruits; lack of adequate people to carry out the administrative work of the club, and keen competition from other clubs in the area. With the numbers taking part in athletics declining sharply during the sixties a situation has arisen where too many clubs have been chasing too few athletes, especially in high density urban areas. Without people to do the work clubs will go into a decline. Without a progressive junior and youth policy clubs will go into a decline.

There are a number of criteria which the management of any athletic club must satisfy to be successful:

(1) Adequate finance to carry out all the club's activities
(2) Adequate management structure
(3) Adequate competition *throughout the year* for all members
(4) Adequate facilities for competition and training
(5) Adequate coaching structure for all membership
(6) Adequate social amenities and functions
(7) A sound junior and youth policy and recruitment programme

Most rural clubs in Britain have a preponderance of young members many of whom are still at school. The main reason for this is that in such areas career and job opportunities are often at a premium, so many young athletes leave the district for colleges or universities and only a small proportion ever return. Clubs should therefore concentrate their junior recruitment efforts upon the local secondary modern and comprehensive schools and upon youngsters who are likely to stay in the area. They must also, to a certain extent, resign themselves to becoming nurseries for the bigger clubs in urban areas.

The problems of the secretary who is setting up a new club or trying to keep one alive are manifold. He or she must take a long, hard look at the task and how they must apportion their effort. The biggest mistake is to try and accomplish everything for this means accomplishing nothing. List the priorities and attack them in order. Top priority is to form some kind of management committee, however small. If there are some junior members, then it is to their parents that the beleagured secretary must look – call a meeting, lay the exact position on the table and call for volunteers. Nine times out of ten some will be forthcoming and if you strike the tenth occasion then the club is not worth continuing with anyway. What is certain is that the problems of club administration in the seventies will increase rather than decrease and that the signs are that people will be more and more unwilling to take on the increasing burdens of honorary work. This may result in a much greater turnover in club officials with people undertaking tasks for a shorter period of time and it may result in further experiments – multi-sports clubs and/or part-time professional administration.

During 1971 this innovation took place in an unlikely quarter, the Torbay Amateur Athletic Club in Devonshire. This club was formed as late as 1970, an amalgam of the Paignton and Torquay Athletic Clubs whose histories go back to the turn of the century. The club is served by a part-time administrator who has a yearly contract. He receives an honorarium of £X per week plus a percentage of profit. This profit is based upon the difference between income and expenditure but not taking into account any money which is spent on assets – equipment etc. In simple terms, the administrator gets a percentage of any money which he *makes*.

This is professionalism in its most basic form and there are many snags which need to be ironed out. In Torbay the contract is so designed that the only loser can, in fact, be the administrator. It has a clause which ensures that if the club's finances are such that they cannot meet their obligations to the administrator he has to waive all right to his money. So only the most dedicated need apply. The first such administrator, Marc Watts, found that there was a natural tendency on the part of some people to leave every task to him because he was receiving some remuneration. He also found that raising money, in that particular area, was not too easy.

It could be from these rather crude beginnings that part-time professional administration in clubs will stem, though it may mean that a club's steady income (club subscriptions) will need to be raised to a much higher level than imagined at the present time. The alternative, in a few years, could be oblivion.

Whichever way a club turns in its efforts to be more efficient and successful it must take into account changing patterns, not only in athletics but in social and political life and be able to be flexible enough to adapt to such changes, survive them and indeed thrive on them.

7

Scheme of management

Once general management and policy have been settled the next priority should be the setting up of a committee structure (see Figure 4). The secretary will soon learn that the secret of success lies in delegation. For a club that has been administratively strong since its inception this will not be difficult but for the man who has had to carry the burden of club organisation over a period of years it is not easy. Often he is frightened to delegate, sometimes he develops an 'indispensable' complex, in a few cases delusions of power have grown. Whatever the reason failure to delegate when the opportunity presents itself can lead to a retarding of progress.

As mentioned earlier, experience has shown that big committees, by their very nature, are incapable of making decisions. Interesting comparisons can be made between the older established clubs in the London area and the committees of the Southern Counties and the Amateur Athletic Associations, all of whom are very large with a surfeit of 'active vice-presidents'. As the full management structure of a club grows, it should meet less and less often if anything positive is to be achieved. Decision making must be left to the sub-committees and individual officers. With a committee structure such as we have indicated there should be no reason for the main committee to meet more than four times a year:

January   Mid-winter review: track season pre-view.
April   Winter season analysis: final track season pre-view.
July   Mid-track season review: winter season pre-view.
September   Track season analysis: final winter pre-view.

The club's annual meeting could then conveniently be held in November.

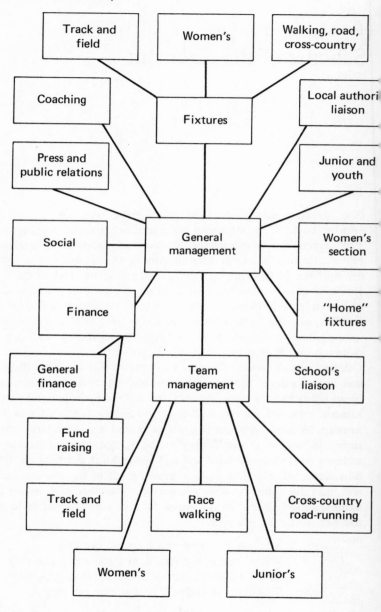

Figure 4

Sub-committees should be kept as small as possible, with each person having an allotted task. The worst committees are those which have a preponderance of members whose sole job is to make comment; the best committees are those whose members all have an allotted task. Taking Figure 4 as a club management structure:

GENERAL MANAGEMENT

Usually this is controlled by three main officers: Chairman, Secretary, Finance Officer. The tasks of the former two are to act as coordinators of the work of the club whilst the latter has overall control of the club's finances.

Chairman

Must be able to handle the committee meetings with tact and firm control but should also take an active interest in club affairs. Some clubs have a limiting clause on the period of time that a chairman may serve, so that the privilege, such as it is, may go to all who deserve it. If such accolades are thought necessary the position of Club President is more suited to such protocol.

Secretary

Often the main driving force. Must be a good day-to-day administrator and have the necessary facilities for carrying out such administration. Need not necessarily be 'steeped' in athletics but obviously must know something about each section's work, the local problems and, most important, have some in-depth knowledge about athletics administration which is one step and more above, i.e. county, area and national administration. He should also be the link with the local authority. The actual type of work carried out by the general secretary of a club will vary according to its size, locality, stage of development – from being a one-man secretary, coach, team manager and general crusader to being the co-ordinator and quiet administrator of a highly functional and positive club committee. As in many walks of life, it can serve a useful purpose if the personalities of the chairman and secretary are somewhat different. Having two ebullient people in these posts can often lead to clash of personality problems whilst having two quiet, basically hard-working characters can have a stultifying effect on the club's development.

Finance Officer

Having someone who is used to dealing with finance is of inestimable value. It is of the utmost importance that the club's finances are strictly controlled, clearly outlined and audited. He must have a strong voice in the annual budgeting and where changes in the club's financial structure are called for his opinions must carry weight. He must also be responsible for fund-raising as well as fund-keeping.

SUB-COMMITTEES OFFICERS
REPRESENTATION ON MANAGEMENT COMMITTEE

One representative of each sub-committee should be represented on the main committee. Where possible there should be adequate representatives of both the male and female sections of the club on the general committee.

COACHING

There must be an overall co-ordinator of club coaching who, if he is so qualified, can also be the chief coach. His job is to make sure that all sections of the club are receiving the coaching assistance that they require. His committee should consist of all those actually doing any coaching and should not need to meet too frequently.

FIXTURES

There should be a main fixtures' secretary, responsible, say, for one of:

(1) Track and field
(2) Women's
(3) Walking, cross-country and road running

with assistant fixtures' secretaries for the other two. He has the important job of co-ordinating all fixtures in terms of travel, home fixtures, booking of local facilities, hiring of transport and of keeping up to date on all major fixtures, i.e. county championships, schools championships, area championships.

LOCAL AUTHORITY LIAISON

Most athletics clubs use facilities provided by the local authority – be it the track, the local school gymnasium or the big park for cross-country races. It is important for the club to have a good liaison and relationship with its local government, to discover the people with whom they should be dealing and set up regular contact.

JUNIOR AND YOUTH SECTION

The life blood of the club and so important to have go-ahead, live-wire people in charge of these sections, preferably those who will have a good understanding of the schools' requirements of the members. Tie up with the Schools Liaison Committee.

WOMEN'S SECTION

Whether there should be an especial women's section is a matter for debate. In a well-integrated club the women athletes should be represented and catered for by the various sub-committees. If this is not the case then it should be one of the immediate objectives of any management committee. However, and alas, this is not the case in a good many clubs and the women athletes feel very much second-class citizens as far as the management committee goes. If nothing else, there is a need for a women's committee to ensure that all their requirements are being met and that they are receiving a fair allocation of club funds. Even when women's athletics is fully integrated into the club there might be a case for a small committee to act as a ginger group.

'HOME' FIXTURES

It is often upon the organisation and success of their 'home' fixtures that a club is judged. This committee needs to get down to the planning of home fixtures very early and will probably be one of the largest of the club's sub-committees.

SCHOOL LIAISON

It is important to tie up with the Junior and Youth Committee and it may be felt that one committee could well fulfil both functions. Liaison should be with:

(1) District/Town Schools Athletic Association
(2) Organiser of Physical Education

(3) Youth Officer
(4) Athletics Master of all the keen local athletics schools

Any schoolmasters within the club should serve on this committee and if others can be coerced in from outside so much the better.

TEAM MANAGEMENT

Asking any one person to act as team manager for all the club all the year round is asking too much. Specialist sections (Road running, race walking) need specialist team managers at club level as much as at international level and every effort should be made towards team managers for:

(1) Track and field (men)
(2) Track and field (women)
(3) Track and field (junior men)
(4) Track and field (junior women)
(5) Cross-country (men)
(6) Cross-country (women)
(7) Road running (men and women)
(8) Race-walking

Obviously when teams combine only one team manager may be needed, but if a full club, junior and senior, men and women, ever travels then there is a real need for four team managers.

FINANCE

This Committee should be split into two sections under the aegis of the Finance Officer. One section should deal with general finance and fund-keeping whilst the other should concern itself with fund-raising.

SOCIAL

Important that the social life of the club throughout the year should flourish with dances, discotheques, supporters trips, excursions to major athletic events and any other function that will help to give the club a warm, social image, not only for its members but for its intending members. Club home fixtures can also give the social committee a good deal of work arranging for refreshments and after-the-events socials.

Often clubs have Supporters Clubs instead of Social Committees who also take on the role of fund raising.

PRESS AND PUBLIC RELATIONS

The image that an athletic club has locally depends on how much coverage the club obtains in the local press – professionally known as 'column inches'. In many cases this is a sadly neglected aspect of club life but it should never be, for most local sports editors are always eager for news, especially during the summer months. Every club should have a Public Relations and Press Officer whose job it is to keep the club's name in the public eye, to feed the local press and, if applicable, radio or television with regular information.

Many clubs also run a club magazine and this can be edited (written and typed!) by a further sub-committee or it can be incorporated into the work of the social committee.

8

Finance and fund raising

This is the most crucial factor in club life. Without adequate finance the most ambitious schemes and plans grind to a halt. The Finance Committee and its officers are probably the most important part of the Management Committee.

However finance does not just involve treasuring the money as the normal title of the officer would imply. It involves budgeting and fund-raising and, in selecting those who will take care of its financial affairs, every club should bear this in mind.

BUDGET

One of the most important Management Committee meetings of the year should involve planning the year ahead in terms of fixtures, home meetings and other major functions which are to be staged – all will involve money. Once the year's programme is settled it is then the job of the Finance Committee to prepare a budget of the year estimating the annual turnover. From Figure 5 it can be seen that for many clubs the turnover is quite high and that this just does not depend on size. Such an estimate should have a contingency sum added to it – for the unexpected expenditure.

For most clubs the major item of the year will be travelling, especially for those involved with League athletics.

CLUB SUBSCRIPTIONS

Again from Figure 5 it can be seen that these are small and often woefully inadequate, a legacy of the pre-war days of athletics when the

CLUB ANALYSIS

Club	No. of active athletes (M)		No. of active athletes (F)		Club Subs.	Total club turnover (£) 1970–1	Approx. dist. travelled in 1971
	J*	S	J*	S			
Torbay AAC	51	47	51	15	30p–u15 50p–u18 £1–o18	£536	2500
Swansea Harriers	55	107	44	39	50p–J* £1–S 50p–u17	£2,062	6,331
Liverpool H & AC	128	94	30	16	£1–u19 £1.50–o19 £1–o19W	£1,920	4,875
City of Leeds AC	148	212	17†	4	25p–J £1–S	£500	1,150

*–for the purpose of this survey a Junior (J) is under 16 years
J–Junior; S–Senior; W–Women; u–under; o–over
†–a newly formed women's section

Figure 5

sport was popular because it was the only one in which even the most impoverished could take part. A great majority of officials cannot lose the 'sixpence in the tin cup' attitude and many clubs' subscriptions have hardly increased over the years, while almost none have kept pace with the cost of living, and so all are really facing difficulties.

What is *well-organised* club athletics worth per week? A cup of British Rail coffee? A half-pint of beer or ten cigarettes? If it is agreed that the answer is yes then club subscriptions should be £2.50 for juniors and £5.00 for seniors.

The vital point is, of course, *well-organised*, but once that is achieved, clubs, and especially new clubs, must put subscriptions at a realistic level. For the more established clubs, however, the position is more difficult. Sharp rises in subscriptions could have an adverse affect on club membership so, again, a realistic approach will bring a medium increase in subscriptions which means that other means of fund-raising have to be found.

WEEKLY FUND RAISING

There are now a number of major firms running weekly competitions from which the individual clubs can gain a maximum proportion of the intake. Such competitions include a weekly Bingo competition in which the club can receive up to 60 per cent of each ticket sold. Thus a club selling 500 tickets at 5p each could make between £650 and £780 per annum. This form of fund-raising is not, of course, confined to athletics and massive amounts of money have been raised by soccer clubs' supporters associations the most notable of which is Glasgow Rangers. Clubs with increasing amounts of annual expenditure should seriously consider such schemes if they are not employing them already. Other forms of competition involving football results, etc. are also common.

SPONSORED RUNS

Sponsored walks, runs and swims have come into vogue in recent years as forms of fund raising. Each participant gets people to sponsor him for so much money, usually a sum per mile and then sets out to complete a certain distance on the day of the sponsored run. Depending upon the number of participants and the novelty this can also raise quite considerable sums of money. Such events, which need careful planning and organising, are usually staged to raise money for a particular event or purpose, such as a new facility or piece of equipment, or travelling to a special event.

200 CLUB

An increasingly popular form of fund-raising competition is the 200 Club. This is a monthly draw type of competition confined to a club with a limit of 200 members. Each pays 25p per week (preferably via a Bankers Order of £13 for the year) giving a total income of £2,600. Each month there is a draw with prizes (say) of £30; £15; £5 and each six months there is a major draw for a Mini car or some equal prize. This will leave a sum of about £1,000 for club funds. If 200 people cannot be found the competition can still be run but, of course, prizes and feed-back to the club are correspondingly reduced.

DANCES AND DISCOTHEQUES

Properly organised, these not only serve as a money-spinner but also enhance the social life and reputation of the club. There is usually some person within a club with a penchant for organising such affairs and to a certain degree he or she should be given their head. It is important to note that such events should be open to the general public and the aim should be to get as big an attendance as possible – the object is to raise money first and have a good social evening second.

RAFFLES, JUMBLE SALES ETC.

The selling of raffle and draw tickets at home fixtures and at other functions, the holding of jumble sales and catering at home fixtures are all a means of raising finance and should be pursued.

Care should be taken with all money-raising schemes that the effort involved will be worth while. Hours spent by large numbers of people giving a yield of £8.65 after expenses is wasted effort.

Further care should be taken that the type of fund-raising pursued falls within the legal limits laid down and if there is any doubt, legal advice should be taken.

EXPENDITURE

In dealing with expenditure the Finance Committee should carefully budget each item and let the organiser know the limit of his budget so that the club does not suddenly find itself involved in a large item of expenditure.

AUDIT

The year's accounts should always be audited by someone qualified from outside the committee and these accounts should be clearly presented at each annual general meeting. At each management meeting a clear statement of the club's financial position should be made.

GRANTS

Numerous dispensations and grants from local and national authorities are available to clubs and the Finance Committee should make themselves fully aware of them.

The one likely to affect most clubs concerns the use of local facilities. In many cases local educational facilities can be obtained at a much cheaper rate if the athletic club is an affiliated youth club. This applies especially to the use of school.gymnasia for winter training and possibly also to the use of school track and field facilities. Because of the size of their junior and youth sections most athletic clubs qualify and contact should be made with the Town/Borough/County Youth Officer concerning affiliation.

The policy with regard to the addition of or improvement to amenities and facilities has changed with the advent of the new executive Sports Council in 1971–2. The government is now encouraging local authorities to give grant-aid for such projects as club houses, major equipment, all-weather facilities and usually this is done on a fifty-fifty basis. The important factor is that clubs must show that they have a twenty-eight-year tenure of the facility that they wish to improve or add to – if local authority tracks are being used they are usually happy to indicate that such tenure is available. Details of such grants can be obtained from the local authority or from the Regional Sports Council.

Clubs should also be aware of the grants which can be made available to the local authority from the government. Basically such grants are available for facilities which can be termed Regional Centres and are available for schemes over £50,000. For new facilities the grant is usually around 15 per cent and for improvement to existing facilities the grant can be around 50 per cent. Again the Regional Sports Council should be contacted for fuller details.

AFFILIATIONS

Whatever branch of the sport is taken up at least one affiliation fee has to be paid. A club that caters for every branch of the sport for both men and women is likely to involve itself with nearly a dozen different fees. Careful study should be made by the club's finance committee of what is obtained for the fee being paid.

9

Junior and youth policy

Without a junior and youth policy a club is likely to regress, especially when it is exposed to any intense form of competition. This is a fact of athletic life which a number of famous clubs have ignored to their cost. A steady recruitment is vital and it must be remembered that the onus for recruitment is upon the club.

Every club should ask the question, what will a youngster look for from us as an athletic *and social* club? The best way to find out is to ask the youngsters themselves. Mostly the answers will take in:

(1) Organisation
(2) Adequate competition
(3) Good social programme

ORGANISATION

One or two people should confine their whole efforts to the junior and youth section and such work requires a dedication and flair at least the equal of those who give so much time to girl guides, boy scouts and youth work generally. Youngsters, of whatever age group, require organising. They like to turn up at 6 pm or whatever time and find someone there ready to coach, teach and generally extol. This is a vital aspect of a good junior policy; a regular attendance at specified times. The younger the group, the more variety they will require during any one session, and so the organisers should plan beforehand a whole collection of training and competitive situations.

It is recommended that for youngsters below the age of thirteen a separate and earlier time for gathering and training should be set aside.

ADEQUATE COMPETITION

This is dealt with in the section on the competition structure. It is important, though, that *every* age group have adequate competition. Even if very young athletes are encouraged they must have experience of competing, though essentially such competitions will be within the club.

GOOD SOCIAL PROGRAMME

Clubs must make every attempt to lose their rather spartan image. Frequent dances, discotheques and other functions will give the club a good social image and athletic clubs could well take a leaf from the books of rugby clubs in this regard. Trips to major meetings also help in encouraging the younger element.

In all approaches to the junior and youth sections it must be remembered that the aim is to encourage youngsters to the sport and not drive them away. Club spirit, the sense of belonging to a 'viable' organisation and a sense of personal achievement are all what young athletes are looking for and what clubs must provide.

PARENT SYNDROME

Anyone who has had any experience of club or school athletics will have had some experience of this and the difficult situation it can create. Often the father is genuinely ambitious for his offspring, but just as often he is as ambitious for himself and any reflected glory which might accrue to him, and so he puts the unfortunate youngster through somewhat drastic training programmes. The greatest problem is that the young athlete is never away from the sport – a bad training session, a poor race or competition and endless post-mortems follow in the car journey home and on into successive meal times. In terms of coaching it is much better to have a separate person with the parent giving much active encouragement in the background and devoting what energies he or she has to the club as a whole.

10

Competition structure

For many years competition for athletic clubs in Britain consisted of a mixture of trophy meetings, casual inter-club meetings, occasional open meetings and various championship meetings and all very laissez-faire. The trophy meetings were entities within themselves and often had odd characteristics – missing out certain field events or with quirks of scoring. Such odd characteristics were originally instituted to make sure that the host club did well. Such a casual (and to many delightful) approach also led to a very casual approach in club administration and in many cases a certain amount of apathy was inevitable.

In 1968 League athletics, for so long the main pattern in Europe, came to Britain and for some clubs the shock was traumatic. By 1971 they system had made great strides, incorporating nearly two-thirds of the clubs in Britain, with a structure topped by the National Athletics League composed of the top twenty-four. Its purpose, initially, was twofold: to rationalise the competitive structure, to give a sense of direction to club life and also to bring about a balance, at club level, between track and field events. After three years both have been achieved to some degree but certainly the impact upon club life has been much greater than could have been imagined. The structure of the League system in Britain is shown in Figure 6. Within is a complete promotion and relegation system so that the clubs in the lower divisions have the incentive to work and improve their status – indeed the way is open for them right through to the National League itself. The system gives, for most fixtures secretaries, a format upon which to build their summer programme. Nationally there are four League meetings during the season but in the Area Leagues there are up to six competitions. In 1973 a national knock-out competition will be introduced

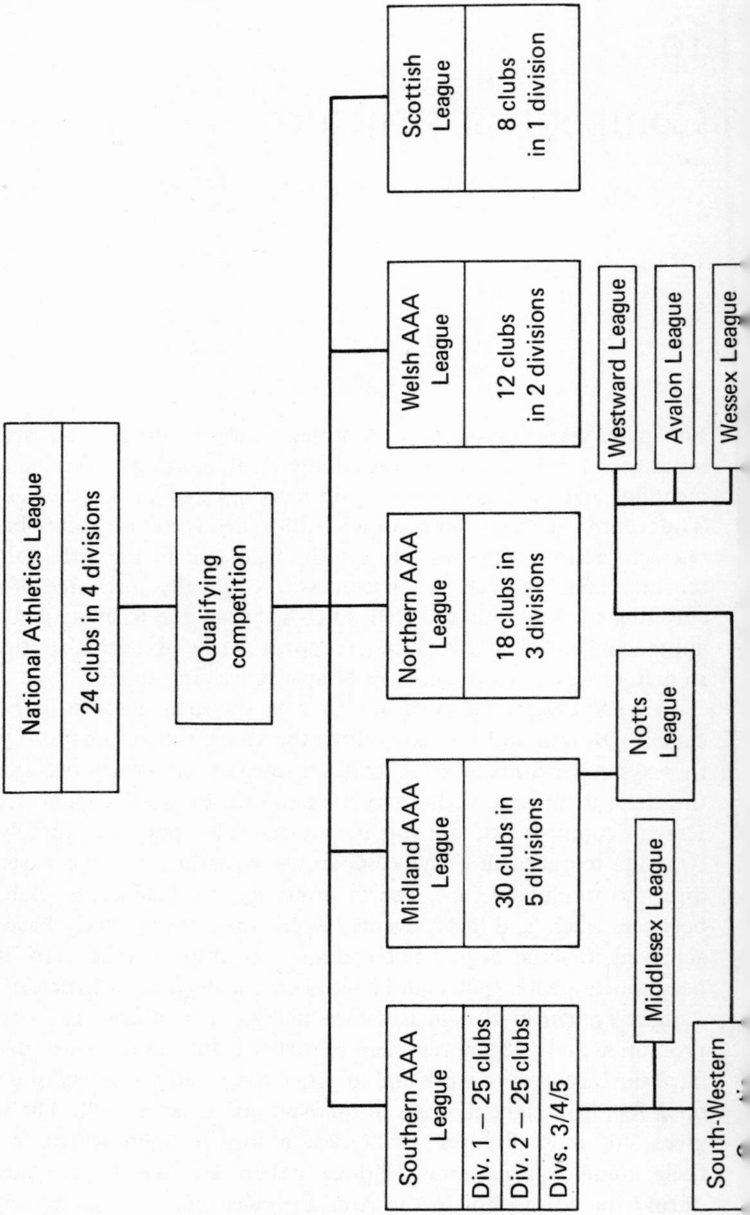
National Athletics League
24 clubs in 4 divisions
Qualifying competition
Scottish League
8 clubs in 1 division
Welsh AAA League
12 clubs in 2 divisions
Northern AAA League
18 clubs in 3 divisions
Midland AAA League
30 clubs in 5 divisions
Southern AAA League
Div. 1 – 25 clubs
Div. 2 – 25 clubs
Divs. 3/4/5
Notts League
Middlesex League
Westward League
Avalon League
Wessex League
South-Western

Figure 6

thus adding a further dimension to a stable competition structure.

For a new club or one that is being revised one of the early tasks is the appointment of a Fixtures Secretary for track and field, the vital cog in the Fixtures Committee indicated in the section on club management. He should then apply to join one of the Area Leagues (see *Appendix*) and also enter the national knock-out competition, which will be very much on a local basis during the early rounds. The dates of the League competitions and the cup rounds are fixed well in advance and this will be the base upon which the Fixtures secretary can build his programme. He will need to look at a number of factors:

(1) Amount of travelling involved in League and cup fixtures

(2) Discover the dates of the major individual meetings i.e. County Championships, Area Championships and if the club has a large junior membership the dates of the relevant Schools Championships

(3) Availability of his home track or stadia and dates of other local major sporting events which he should try to avoid e.g. local Football League fixtures, Rugby fixtures etc., County Cricket matches

When he has ascertained these facts he must then consider the types of meeting that the club wishes to take part in and to stage.

Some clubs believe in staging massive quantity meetings which cater for every event, for every age group, men and women, and which begin about 10 am and end as the sun dips over the horizon after one hundred and thirty-four events – as the exhausted secretary will proudly tell you. Such meetings undoubtedly have their place, especially for a club with a large quantity of young athletes but they are, generally, not recommended. Inter-club meetings should have some discernible shape about them so that the spectator can quite easily gauge what is going on. The fixtures secretary, in conjunction with his assistants, should join together only certain age groups at one meeting. He should group his ages thus:

Men	*Women*
Senior/Junior	Seniors/Intermediates
Youth/Boys	Juniors/Minors
Minors	

If he wishes to stage all track and field events in his inter-club meeting, he should aim at excepting, perhaps, the 10,000 metres, and he should expect to combine at one meeting only two of the above groups – i.e. Senior/Junior Men with Senior/Intermediate Women with the addition of one or two events for Minors of both sexes. During the season he should aim at catering for all the above at regular intervals and when it is complete his 'fixture calendar' may look something like Figure 7.

CLUB FIXTURE CALENDAR

SUMMER (MEN AND WOMEN)

April

Last two weeks
Club Championships
Possible early Inter-club Meeting

May

1st Week
Club Championships
Inter-Club Meeting   Senior/Junior (M) and Senior/Intermediate (W)
National Knock-Out Cup
2nd Week
Open Meeting for Youths/Boys/Minors (M) and Junior/Minors (W)
National League/Area League/Women's League
3rd Week
Inter-Club Meeting   Youths/Boys (M) and Junior/Minors (W)
County/Sub-area Championships   (M) and (W)
4th Week
Area Championships   (W)
County Championships   (M)
Open Meeting: Minors
5th Week
Home Trophy Meeting   Senior/Junior (M) and
                                      Senior/Intermediate (W)
Inter-County Championships   (M)

June

1st Week
National League/Area League/Womens League
Inter-Club Meeting: Women – Senior/Intermediate

2nd Week
Inter-Club Meeting   Senior/Junior (M)
Open Graded Meeting   All age groups (W)
County Schools
3rd Week
Trophy Meetings
Open Meeting   Minors (M) and (W)
4th Week
Area Championships   (M)
Inter-Club Meeting   Senior and Junior (W)
Open Graded Meeting   All age groups (M)

July

1st Week
National/Area/Women's Leagues
National Schools Championships
2nd Week
Women's National Championships
Men's Inter-Club or Trophy Meeting
Open Meeting   Junior and Youth and Minors (M)
3rd Week
Men's National Championships
Women's Inter-Club   Senior and Intermediates
4th Week
National/Area/Women's Leagues
Inter-Club Match   Youths and Boys (M)
Open Meeting   All age groups (W)

1st Week

Inter-Club Match   Juniors and Youths (M)
National or Area Leagues or semi-finals of Knock-Out Cup
2nd Week
Inter-Club   Senior Men and Senior Women
Open Meeting
3rd Week
Open Graded Meeting
4th Week
Inter-Club   Senior and Junior and Senior and Intermediate Women

Figure 7

The important factor is to have plenty of variety ensuring that all club members, irrespective of age and sex, obtain adequate competition.

The great danger, with the coming of League and Cup athletics, *is that other sections of the club will be neglected* and this is something to avoid at all costs. On League and Cup days, Fixtures Secretaries and Team Managers should be conscious of what competition other club members are finding that day.

Often a club traditionally has a big open meeting which it stages each year and these always add a dimension to the fixture lists of the particular area. The Kinnaird and Sward Trophy meetings are staged by the Polytechnic Harriers; the Melbourne Trophy by Liverpool Harriers and AC; the Bracknell Relays are run by Bracknell AC and young athletes' meetings are staged at places like Camberley and Solihull. Other clubs run decathlon competitions and other specialist events.

Those serving the junior sections of the club will look to see if there are any schools locally who take athletics seriously and try to arrange fixtures.

Events for all those in a club are as follows:

MEN

Senior	Junior	Youths	Boys	Minors
100m	100m	100m	100m	100m
200m	200m	200m	200m	200m
400m	400m	400m	400m	
800m	800m	800m	800m	800m
1,500m	1,500m	1,500m	1,500m	
5,000m	3,000m			
10,000m				
110mH	110mH	100mH	80mH	70mH
400mH	400mH			
3,000m St.	2,000m St.	1,500m St.		
4 × 100mR	4 × 100mR	4 × 100mR	4 × 100mR	4 × 100mR
4 × 400mR	4 × 400mR			
HJ	HJ	HJ	HJ	HJ
PV	PV	PV	PV	PV
LJ	LJ	LJ	LJ	LJ
TJ	TJ	TJ	TJ	
SP	SP	SP	SP	SP
DT	DT	DT	DT	
HT	HT	HT	HT	
JT	JT	JT	JT	

WOMEN

Senior	Intermediate	Junior	Minor
100m	100m	100m	100m
200m	200m	200m	150m

400m	400m		
800m	800m	800m	
1,500m	1,500m		
3,000m	3,000m		
100mH	80mH	75mH	70mH
200mH			
4 × 100mH	4 × 100mH	4 × 100mH	4 × 100mH
4 × 400mH	4 × 400mH		
HJ	HJ	HJ	HJ
LJ	LJ	LJ	LJ
SP	SP	SP	SP
DT	DT	DT	
JT	JT	JT	

The pattern of club competition will change during the seventies. Already the support for County Championships is dwindling fast and with the pattern of local government about to change one may well see this type of meeting dwindling away and the pattern being:

(1) Club Championships
(2) National, Area and Local League and Cup structure
(3) Sub-area Championships
(4) Area Championships
(5) National Championships

Apart from inter-club and trophy meetings there are other types of competition that could be staged:

OPEN GRADED MEETINGS

These offer a wide opportunity for *all standards* of athletes and also enable them to compete against others of a similar standard. In the men's 1,500 metres, for instance, three graded races might be run:

Grade 1   Competitors better than 4 minutes 12 seconds
Grade 2   Competitors better than 4 minutes 25 seconds
Grade 3   Competitors who have not achieved 4 minutes 25 seconds

and so on. Such meetings could be attached to National Association standard (see the appropriate handbooks) thus giving a further incentive to the athletes. Prior application to apply standards to your meeting should be made to the appropriate association. Though clubs can and do stage such meetings it should be the type of meeting that County Associations or whatever structure takes their place should stage.

These are essentially meetings for participants rather than spectators and thus the organisers can go for a fair amount of quantity – though this will mean very careful organisation.

NOVICE EVENINGS

Most clubs in Poland put aside one evening each week during the season for a novice meeting when anyone at all can come along and have a go at any event that is being staged. Advance notice of such evenings is given in the press and with advertising. Athletics is full of stories of champions who have taken up the event, even the sport, by accident. The most classic British case is that of Arthur Rowe who picked up a shot and putted it idly whilst waiting to bat in a cricket match. So, opportunity must be given.

OTHER TYPES OF MEETING

All sorts of novel innovations of the normal track and field meeting have been successfully carried out. The Kirkby Sevens, where each club is allowed seven competitors; the Stretford League, a series of open meetings where individuals compete against each other on a League basis and invitation events at football matches are all examples of these. The latter has been successfully tried out by a number of people, notably the British Milers Club and Sutton and Cheam Harriers. Invitation athletic events can easily be staged at half-time at football matches and many good football clubs are glad of the opportunity to fill the gap.

So the Fixtures Secretary can be a very busy man or woman, and though most of his work is done through the winter and spring months, last minute problems will also keep him active during the summer. Points he should note are:

Correspondence
Write well in advance; suggest dates, age groups and events. Find out something about your prospective opposition in advance, e.g., not much point in offering a fixture for junior women if the other club has none. Always have as full a programme as possible and do not encourage the exclusion of such events as hammer and pole vault. Keep a copy of all correspondence. Be prompt in replying to letters.

Scoring

Keep to conventional scoring patterns and avoid complicated methods which mean that the majority of spectators and athletes are completely baffled from about event three onwards. Conventional scoring patterns are:

DUAL MEETINGS
Individual events   5 3 2 1
Relays   5 2
TRIANGULAR MEETINGS
Individual events   7 5 4 3 2 1
Relays   10 7 3
SIX-A-SIDE MATCHES
Individual events   12 10 8 6 5 4 (A strings)
                        8 6 4 3 2 1   (B strings)*
Relays   12 10 8 6 5 4

*in six-a-side matches first and second string separate events will be required in events up to 1,500 metres. In the longer distance events and the field events all the competitors compete together and the first scoring athlete automatically scores A string points.

Try to ensure that every competitor scores for his club.

Officials
See 'Organising a sports day'.

Organisation
See that your opponents have every piece of information they require well in advance. They need to know:

(1) Time of starting
(2) Timetable of events
(3) Scoring systems
(4) Numbers allotted to their club(s) and if these (and pins) are supplied
(5) Exact dates of age groupings
(6) Any restrictions in the rules of the competition (restricted number of events per athlete)
(7) Numbers and types of officials you require from them
(8) Refreshment information
(9) Social function information
(10) Directions to the venue – by coach/car or public transport

and for away matches

(1) Try to ensure that the team travels together for it adds considerably to club spirit. If a coach is to be booked, go to a reputable firm, tell him your requirements and get quotations – it will certainly pay you to approach a number of coach firms. Find out from him how long the journey will take, then add one hour to allow for bad traffic conditions and adequate warming-up time for the competitors in the early events

(2) Make sure that there will be adequate provision for the taking of equipment, especially fibre-glass poles

(3) Allow time for a social stop on the way back if there is no social function at the venue

(4) Let the competitors know well in advance how much the trip will cost and ensure collection of fares on the coach

Fixtures secretaries and committees should always liaise closely with the finance committee and with the team management and at the close of each season should meet together to review the past season and think ahead to the next in the light of what has been learnt.

CROSS-COUNTRY AND ROAD RUNNING

As Britain has more tradition, more distance-runners and more winter open fixtures than probably any other country in the world the task of the Fixtures Secretary in winter is not too arduous. Much of what has been said about summer fixtures applies also here but in terms of actual matches the numbers are very much smaller. Certainly the dates of the County, Area and National Championships must be noted well in advance: such dates are now standardised by the various cross-country unions. In addition he will also need to know the dates of other time-honoured fixtures such as the South of the Thames, North of the Thames and some of the major road races. Cross-country leagues abound throughout the country for both men and women and membership of one of these, together with runners taking part in a whole host of traditional fixtures, leaves very little room for additions. The Fixtures Secretary in winter must review his established fixtures annually and make additions, where necessary, for all age groups, making sure, once more, that every part of his club's winter section is catered for. As with the summer fixtures, a close liaison should be kept with the Finance Committee and team management and a review made at the end of each winter to see what changes and improvements can be made.

RACE WALKING

Most clubs rely on the excellent network of fixtures which are set up by the Race Walking Association and any new club contemplating a walking section is well advised to contact the RWA who will give them full information about fixtures. Encouragement of walking should be maintained by the inclusion of a track walk in some inter-club track fixtures.

SCHOOL-CLUB CLASHES

These must be avoided at all costs and the closer the liaison between local schools and the club the less chance there is of this occurring. In the end, though, it must always be remembered that in all circumstances *the school has first claim* and that no amount of arguing and haggling can change this fact.

INDOOR ATHLETICS

Competitive indoor athletics take place in Britain mostly at the RAF station at Cosford, near Wolverhampton and at the Bell Indoor Sports Centre in Perth in Scotland. At RAF St Athan in south Wales some indoor athletics takes place on the floor of a large hanger there.

For the field event athletes and the sprinters indoor competition can act as a great incentive during the winter months and for the open meeting at Cosford in November and December each year entries of well over 1,000 are normal necessitating up to twenty odd races for each event.

Clubs should think carefully about running coach trips to the indoor meetings and thus adding a dimension to their competitive structure.

11

Administration of a track and field meeting

Administering a track and field athletic meeting means organising one of the, if not the, most complicated of sporting occasions. Not only can there be well over one hundred events involved but also, as in the case of some major schools meetings, over 1,500 competitors.

Meetings vary from the small club championship meeting which can take place on a fairly casual basis one evening, to an international invitation meeting involving overseas athletes, 20,000 plus spectators and international press and television coverage. In recent years the Coca-Cola Invitation Meeting organised by the International Athletes Club, and the Sward Trophy Meeting organised by the Polytechnic Harriers have been prime examples of clubs organising their own international meetings similar to those which are quite common in Europe and the United States.

Because of the variety of the meetings, prospective club organisers are recommended to read also the section on 'Organising a sports day' which although at the level of a school sports day has much that will be appropriate to the organiser of the small club meeting. In this section we have assumed a large trophy or international meeting is to be administrated and, again, organisers must take from it what they feel is appropriate to the type of meeting or match they are dealing with. It is a mistake to assume that the bigger, internationally-orientated meetings are the most difficult to organise. Probably the most difficult are those that attempt to cater for everybody and unfortunately these are usually the most chaotic. What is clear is that, regardless of the size and importance of the meeting, the same basic outlines apply and the problems are often identical. If there is one common denominator for all it is attention to detail.

FIELD EVENT PROGRESS IN BRITAIN

Showing number of performances achieved in Divisions One, Two and Three of the National Athletics League equal to or better than the standard* indicated (Compiled by Peter Matthews)

Event	Standard	Year		
		1969**	*1970*	*1971*
High jump	1.80m 5′11″	21	32	39
Pole vault	3.40m 11′1†″	25	37	46
Long jump	6.75m 22′1†″	28	37	41
Triple jump	13.60m 44′7½″	47	47	60
Shot put	13.15m 43′1†″	39	56	56
Discus Throw	40.00m 131′3″	51	62	66
Hammer throw	40.00m 131′3″	44	58	60
Javelin throw	56.50m 185′4″	40	46	47
Totals		295	375	415

* standard approximates to 100th best performer in UK 1971
** In 1969 only three fixtures were held. Figures adjusted to four
† In Division 1 in 1971 there were only three pole vault competitions instead of four

Figure 8

MEETING ORGANISING COMMITTEE

In the preliminary planning of the event it is necessary to set up an executive committee composed of a *small* number of individuals (say four to six people) who are experienced in the organisation of a meeting and who will be assuming quite important roles later in the organisation. This committee should gather at least six to eight months in advance to lay out the framework of organisation, select a date – though this may well have had to be decided before – and appoint a Meeting

Manager and/or Director. They may also discuss, in general terms, the type of meeting visualised.

MEETING MANAGER OR DIRECTOR

He is the kingpin around which the meeting revolves and upon whom, ultimately success or failure will depend. Whether he should undertake both direction of the pre-meeting administration and of the meeting itself is a matter for the organising committee, though generally such a dual appointment does ensure continuity. He will assume the greatest responsibility for the running of the meeting, will have at his finger-tips up-to-date knowledge of every facet of the organisation and be able to step in immediately any crises develop. He must have good administrative ability, be able to delegate easily, be able to pick the right men for the right job, have a flair for public relations and publicity and be able to talk freely and coherently with the communications media. One of the trends of the seventies will be for such meeting directors to be appointed on a professional basis.

PRE-MEETING SUB-COMMITTEES (see Figure 9)

As early as is possible the Meeting Organising Committee should appoint sub-committee chairmen who will be responsible to the Meeting Director. Once these are appointed they will form the Meeting Organising Committee which will meet periodically – say once a month – to assess progress. As can be seen from the figure eleven such committees are suggested, though obviously the number and composition will be flexible according to the type of meeting. Here is a suggested brief outline of the duties of each:

Awards

What awards and trophies are being given? This will depend on the type of sponsorship involved – and for the really big meetings some form of sponsorship is essential. Are these awards to be on a permanent or perpetual basis? What sort of budget is put aside for this item? If there is no sponsor, will it be possible to get trophies or prizes donated locally? Will any trophies awarded have to be engraved? Will any need insuring? Provide a signature book so that cups and trophies are signed for. Send out letters well in advance asking for the return of trophies won the previous year. Arrange with a firm in the

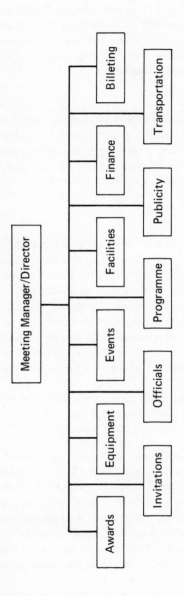

Figure 9

area to put the trophies on display in a window, together with action shots of some of the athletes who will be competing. At the recent European Championships in Helsinki and the Commonwealth Games in Edinburgh, many shops had displays in their windows and there is no reason why this could not be done locally.

Equipment

This committee should survey the types of equipment needed for the meeting and check the equipment which is available at the stadium well in advance. List the events which are being staged and the equipment needed for each. Make sure that all equipment is official and complies with IAAF or the rules of the National Association concerned. A sample check list is given in the *Appendix*.

Events

The events committee should decide what form the programme should take, limitations of entries, whether the meeting should be open or by invitation, deadline for closing entries, who will be the Events Secretary, how the meeting will be advertised in respect of receiving entries. If the meeting should be an inter-club one, the committee should also decide on the points-scoring system to be used for submission to the main Organising Committee. The committee should also be responsible for the collection of entry forms, the seeding of heats, drawing of the lanes (preferably this should be done in advance) and preparing a list of competitors' numbers.

The events committee should also draw up a time schedule of events which will be incorporated into the official programme. This is a vital aspect of pre-meeting planning. Some factors to consider:

(1) In a meeting where large numbers of spectators are involved the meeting must have a set time to begin and the first event should be one that can make an impact. Some organisers tend to let their meetings have a 'drifting' type of start where odd events that do not warrant a place in the main part of the programme are put on, e.g., a 10,000 metres track walk or schoolboys' and girls' invitation events or relay races. This may be well and good at local level but as the meeting grows in status and wider appeal, a good start is essential.

(2) Gaps should be sufficient to present each event as a 'package-deal':

(a) Presentation of athletes

(b) Competition

(c) Announcement of result and presentation of awards

but should not be so long as to leave frequent periods of almost complete inactivity. If there are unavoidable gaps between track events make sure that there are field events being staged which the public can enjoy and which can be spotlighted by the presentation team.

(3) Times of local transport should be taken into consideration when deciding on the timing of the start and the length of the programme. Not many people arrive to watch a meeting much before 2 pm and if the meeting goes beyond about 5.30 pm there will be a steady drift-away of spectators. In terms of an inter-club, or international matches where a team result is an essential part of the meeting, it is important that the great majority of spectators go away knowing the match result – if you want them to come back again.

(4) If you have television coverage of the meeting then an early tie-up on their requirements is essential, especially if part of the meeting is to be scheduled 'live'. The TV company and organisers will need to equate viewing time with the star events of the programme. In this respect it will be important that the meeting runs to time!

(5) Sufficient time should be allowed for athletes to compete in more than one event and if heats are involved sufficient time should be allowed to enable semi-finalists/finalists to recover. Recommendations in this regard are:

Up to and including 200 metres   45 minutes

201 to 1,000 metres inclusive   90 minutes

Over 10,000 metres   3 hours

A typical meeting timetable is shown in the *Appendix*.

One of the most exciting meetings, from a spectator's viewpoint, ever to be held in Britain was the 1971 Coca-Cola Invitation Meeting at the Crystal Palace National Recreation Centre, under floodlights, in September. Though the essential common denominator, attention to detail, had been neglected to a certain extent, this was not obvious to the 12,000 or so spectators who revelled in a highly dramatic and emotion-packed evening. Each race was more climactic than the one before and at the end there were crowd scenes rarely seen in British athletics. The meeting unfolded thus:

7.30 pm   *1,000 metres (Men)*   field includes Tom Saisi, world class Kenyan 800 metres runner

7.50 pm   *100 metres (Women)*   top British sprinters versus Stephanie Berto of Canada, a Commonwealth and Pan-American medalist

8.05 pm   *Len Hatton Mile (Men)*   in an Olympic-type field Ben Jipcho of Kenya beats European champion Francesco Arese of Italy in well under four minutes

8–9 pm   *Pole vault*   world-record holder soars over 17 feet and sets a new British all-comers record

8.35 pm   Kip Keino runs the third fastest 5,000 metres of all time beating Alvarez of Spain. David Black of Britain sets a new world junior record in the same race

8.55 pm   *Lillian Board Memorial 800 metres*   Shela Carey beats European champion Vera Nikolic from Yugoslavia with a grandstand finish

9.15 pm   Stephanie Berto wins the women's 200 metres

9.20 pm   *3,000 metres steeplechase*   David Bedford beats Andy Holden in a highly dramatic race and sets a new British record

The lesson for a clear-cut open invitation meeting is clear:

(1) The meeting should be fairly short (2 to $2\frac{1}{2}$ hours)

(2) Each race should be carefully selected so that the spectators are kept entertained for the duration and so that the excitement can gradually mount (in the above meeting there was the additional factor that the spectators knew that Bedford, the hero of the 1971 big crowds, was going to run his second-ever steeplechase and had vowed publicly to beat the British record)

(3) Presentation of the meeting should be to the whole crowd

Facilities

The committee should examine the stadium carefully beforehand, remembering the criteria necessary for the setting up of records. Such inspection should be carried out with the appropriate authorities represented. The following should be noted:

(1) Is the track of standard dimensions and has it the necessary certificate from the appropriate governing body

(2) Are the field event areas located so that the meeting programme can be staged as laid down, e.g. high jump and javelin etc?

(3) Are high-jumping and pole-vaulting landing areas of sufficient standard to allow for vaulting up to 17 and 18 feet and Fosbury Flop high-jump technique? Are the shot, discus and hammer circles adequate and can they be staged in the centre of the arena? Are the triple-jump take-off boards a sufficient distance from the pit for top line competitions?

(4) Are all markings on the track clear?

(5) Where will the warm-up area be for the athletes?

(6) Is the steeplechase water-jump area up to standard and completely safe?

(7) Is changing accommodation adequate?

(8) Are refreshments and lavatory facilities adequate for the anticipated number of spectators?

(9) Are there sufficient numbers of entry points open on the day for the anticipated number of spectators?

(10) Will there be sufficient car parking space?

(11) Will there be sufficient undercover accommodation available in case of inclement weather?

(12) If large numbers of spectators are visualised, are there any bottle-neck points for traffic locally that might need police attention and should certain spectators or ticket-holders be routed differently to the track? Is the normal local transport system going to be able to cope?

The committee should also appoint two highly experienced men as clerk of the course (track) and clerk of the course (field).

Finance

The committee should work out the budget of the meeting well in advance. If the meeting has a sponsor then this, of course, should be presented to him. Such a budget should include: printing, advertising, equipment, prizes, billeting, refreshments, before and/or after the meeting functions, transport of competitors, travelling expenses etc. The Finance Officer should be a person well-versed in money matters and preferably with previous experience. He can either open a Meeting Account with a bank or he can charge items to the organising association or club within the limit of the budget laid down. Any extra expense would require the full approval of the Organising Committee.

The committee should also handle ticket sales, select suitable personnel to man the entry points to the stadium (if these are not provided), to sell programmes, man the car parks and provide tickets etc. for all these purposes. It may be necessary at some stadia to provide signs indicating the various prices of admission. If reserved seats or guests enclosures are provided, the committee should make sure that there are ushers or a reception committee for VIPs.

Advance-ticket sales must also be organised, ways and means, price reductions (if any), available outlets such as shops etc., bonus schemes for club members who sell tickets and a system of collecting ticket money. A system of collecting the 'gate-money' on the day must also be clearly evolved.

Payment of expenses to athletes and officials should be the responsibility of one man and the approved expense forms of the various governing bodies should be used. Any demand by an athlete or official *which the organisers feel is unreasonable* should be placed before the appropriate governing body.

Billeting

For meetings lasting for more than one day, or where officials and athletes have to travel from abroad or long distances there will be considerable problems concerning the visitors' billeting and feeding. In some cases this is achieved by billeting them in the homes of club or association members, but where no such facility is available or is considered inadequate, hotel accommodation must be used. The organisers should accept complete responsibility for such billeting and use a local hotel that is well-known, comfortable and reasonable. The manager should be informed of any problems involved well in advance – odd meal-times due to the timing of races, particulars of competitors coming from abroad. If the meeting is at a week-end, a reduced rate may be obtained. The organisers should meet the account *en bloc* rather than go through an elaborate process of each athlete or official paying and then claiming back. If any after-meeting function is planned (either social or banquet), it might be a good idea to use the hotel facilities, thus cutting down on transport problems.

Invitations and athletes from abroad

Working with the events committee, invitations to individual athletes from abroad should be made early and must be made, under IAAF ruling, either through the British Amateur Athletics Board in Britain or the Board Luthchleas Na h'Eireann in the Republic of Ireland. The most successful invitation meetings are staged where a few very good and well-known track and field stars are invited for certain events. The public is, and always has been, attracted to the 'big-name confrontation' type of event – Chataway versus Kuts; Pirie versus Zatopek; Ryun against Keino – or to the outstanding personality such as Derek Ibbotson, Gordon Pirie or David Bedford. Some athletes may be the greatest in the world but have no box-office appeal whatsoever.

This committee can also decide what local dignatories should be invited – the Mayor, local MPs, top athletic officials etc. One of these could be asked to open the meeting (though this is usually rather a ponderous business) and if awards are to be presented, most of the invited guests should be asked to take part. A letter should be sent to all those on the complimentary list and those replying should be sent a pair of tickets. Often a special section of the stand is set aside for this purpose. If the meeting has a sponsor, he will require some special function either before the meeting or afterwards in order to entertain, in the first instance, any special VIPs he may have invited. This is nearly always dealt with by the sponsor's public relations department.

Officials

If top officials are required, a letter should be sent to the Area Officials Committee concerned asking for the meeting to be placed on their 'availability lists'. This must be done by the previous November at the latest. The Area Officials Secretary will return a list of officials who have signified their willingness to officiate at the meeting and the committee should immediately send out formal invitations. Alternatively, lists of county or district officials can be obtained and they can then be approached direct. Referees and other major officials should be selected in conjunction with the Officials Committee of the governing body concerned. Some few weeks before the meeting each official should be sent a package which contains

(1) Entry ticket and one complimentary
(2) Timetable of events
(3) List of all officials
(4) Directions to the track or stadium
(5) The time officials should report and to whom

Programme

This should be carefully planned in terms of content and advertising. Should it be a printed programme? How much should it be sold for?

If a printed programme can be afforded, it should look attractive and have sufficient information to serve as a souvenir of the meeting. It should include:

(1) Timetable of events
(2) List of all officials
(3) Names and affiliations of all competitors (with christian names if possible)
(4) An up-to-date best performance for each competitor (this can usually be obtained with help from the National Union of Track Statisticians – see *Appendix*)
(5) Appropriate records: world, national, all-comers, meeting and track plus any relevant standards e.g. Olympic Games, European Championships, European Indoor etc.
(6) Adequate space for writing in the results of the first six competitors – or eight for the very large meetings
(7) Adequate space for noting programme changes
(8) Photographs of the leading competitors
(9) A background article or two on the meeting with spotlight on some big events of the past or outstanding personalities who have competed at the meeting
(10) If an inter-club/nation match previous results of the contest and a page for noting the team scores after various events
(11) A blank page for autographs

Advertising should be the key to a successful programme and realistic charges should be made. Study other meeting programmes to see who is advertising and do the same with the programmes of other local sporting events.

If there is a sponsor consult him about the format of the programme and what he would like included. The cover should be attractive and eye-catching and often it is a good idea to equate poster and programme-cover design.

Publicity

The committee must have a budget to work to so as to assess the feasibility of press publicity, press luncheons, advertising. If the meeting is of national or even international significance and sponsored, then a press conference *cum* luncheon is a good idea. Make sure that you have something worthwhile to announce – 'We are going to stage a meeting on 21 June' is hardly enough to set alight the back pages of

WAAA Championships 1971;
E. Tittel (West Germany)
leads Rita Ridley (Essex
LAC)

Olympic Games, Mexico 1968;
Bob Beamon (USA) making
his world-record long jump

European Championship, Helsinki 1971; Barbara Inkpen (Great Britain), silver medallist in the high jump

Opposite AAA Indoor Championship, 29 January 1972; David Bedford leading Ian Stewart in the 3,000 metres

50th International CCC at Cambridge, 18 March 1972 – the last in its present form; Ian Stewart (Scotland) leading Haddou Jaddour (Morocco), Gaston Roclarts (France), the eventual winner, and Noel Tijou (France) in the senior race

National CCC, Parliament Hill, 6 March 1965; just after the start of the senior race, the biggest cross-country field in the world

Modern pole-vault landing area at RAF Cosford

Indoor track, Bell Sports Centre, Perth

Above and opposite: Coca Cola/IAC Meeting, Crystal Palace, 10 September 1971; C. Papanicolaou (Greece), the then world record holder during the pole-vaulting

Olympic stadium, Mexico, 1968; 'Tartan' track heralds beginning of all-weather era

5/4 in. thick Sitka Spruce indoor track, Philadelphia Inquirer Games, Convention Hall, Philadelphia

the top daily newspapers. Have a list of athletes who are being invited and who have accepted. Advance press publicity, whether national or local, is essential and regular hand-outs should be issued. Displaying trophies in windows; interviews on local radio and/or television, car stickers, posters, pretty girls handing out leaflets on the morning of the meeting are all ideas that could be pursued. Have photographs of some of the outstanding competitors available for the press and for display in local shops; get as many 'stories' as possible i.e. stories of human interest value and not athletics statistics. Use a roving PA on the morning of the meeting; plug local interest. Try and get local personalities to show an interest. The aim of the publicity committee must be to ensure that no one living within a certain radius of the meeting is unaware that it is taking place.

Transportation
This involves meeting athletes and officials travelling in from abroad (at the airport or seaport) or just at the local railway station and ensuring that they have adequate transport during their stay i.e. from the hotel or billet to training facilities and to the meeting and finally back again to the terminal from which they were picked up. The importance of this committee and the magnitude of its work will depend on the size of the meeting.

Meeting presentation
As opposed to the planning of the meeting a special committee should be involved with the presentation of the meeting on the day.
As stated earlier it may be decided that the Meeting Manager and Meeting Director will both be the same person to ensure continuity.

Meeting Director
As the name implies, the Meeting Director directs the actual track and field programme, consults with and advises the key officials working on the various events and directs the activities of the presentation committee. The Meeting Director is in complete charge of the presentation of the meeting before and during the programme. In a large meeting, it may be as well to appoint one or two assistants.
During the meeting the Director should be with the presentation committee. From here he can control the pace of the meeting and with a good communications system can be in instant contact with the main technical officials should the need arise. He should act in this sense very much as the producer/director of a TV programme would act.

Presentation committee

The actual track and field programme is divided into two parts – one is concerned with the actual presentation of the meeting and the other is concerned with technical officiating (see Figure 10).

PRESENTATION

Any meeting of standard should have a presentation team which consists of:

(1) Meeting Director
(2) Commentators (2)
(3) Communications Co-ordinator
(4) Communications Stewards
(5) Ceremonial Stewards
(6) Press Liaison Officer
(7) Recorders
(8) Statistical Co-ordinator

Commentators

The one-time nomenclature of announcer is now very much out of date. Though actual TV/Radio type commentaries are out of context at an athletics meeting, it is, nevertheless, the commentators' job to present the meeting to the mass of the spectators gathered and to keep them informed of events which are occurring or are about to occur. Selection of commentators is of vital importance, for they can make or mar a meeting. There is a thin line between worthwhile and informative commentary and talking too much. As a general guide, commentators should appreciate that the public have come to watch athletes and not to hear them talk about it. Commentators require a knowledge of athletics, a clear, well-modulated voice, an urbane temperament, a sense of humour.

The audience to whom they are communicating usually consists of the spectators – who have usually paid to see athletic entertainment – the participating athletes, the officials, representatives of the mass media i.e. press/radio/TV. The great majority, however, will be spectators and it is to them that their main attention should be directed. Spectators can be broken down as follows:

(1) Those with a love for, and a great knowledge of athletics
(2) The athletics enthusiasts who attend a fair number of meetings

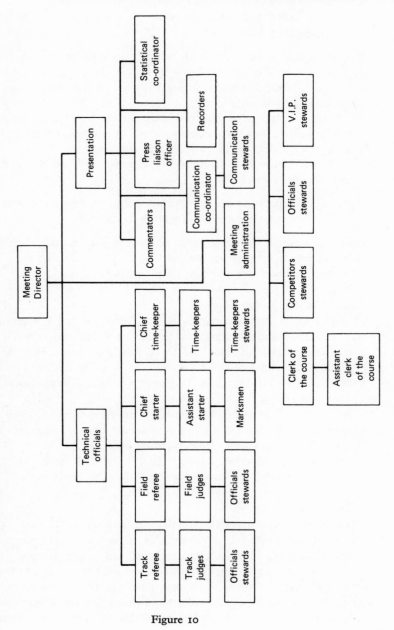

Figure 10

(3) The casual and novice spectator who will have little in-depth knowledge of the sport

The proportions will vary from meeting to meeting and it is the difficult task of the commentators to be able to impart information to all three groups without causing irritation to one section, usually those in the first section.

What is essential, is for the commentators to be fed as much information as possible about the competitors well in advance to enable them to carry out the detailed preparation that is necessary.

Each commentator's role should be pre-specified and the work is usually divided up into:

(1) General presentation commentator, also covering track events
(2) Results commentator also covering field events

A further essential is a good public address system and this should be checked well in advance by the Meeting Director. Go to a reputable firm that you know will give you a good service.

Communications co-ordinator
He acts as chief 'back-up' man to the two commentators. It is essential that a speedy communications service can be maintained between the events that are taking place and the presentation team. In order of preference this communications service can be carried out by, walkie-talkie link (preferably), field telephones or track communications system, runners.

It is the task of the communications co-ordinator to control the various stewards, their input of information and to assess such information to the commentators – *who still might not use it.*

However all information must always be fed back with the commentator having the final say on what information he uses.

Communications stewards
These can vary from experienced walkie-talkie operators standing out by the event and feeding back winning times, quick results, round-by-round summaries of field events, changes in height in pole vault competititions, outstanding performances in field events etc. to young school children operating as runners from the various events to the presentation team. The latter will not, of course, provide a very speedy or communicative service. Each however has to link up in a friendly

manner with the technical officials dealing with the events and his main concern is *not* to pester them!

Ceremonial stewards
If victory or presentation ceremonies are required these should take place as soon as the event is finished, in order to present a whole package-event to the public. After the event, the first three, or whatever may be decided, should be taken by a ceremonial steward to the presentation plinth where another steward has forewarned the person making the presentation, selected the prizes and awards to be made and informed the presentation team.

It must be this team and, probably, the Meeting Director who will make the final decision as to the exact moment when the ceremony will take place. Some form of fanfare should precede the ceremony (providing there are not too many).

Press liaison steward
Another essential cog in the presentation team. His job is to keep the press well informed as the meeting unfolds and ideally he should be able to receive the same messages as the communications co-ordinator. He can either have a second 'master' receiver or the co-ordinator has a carbon pad to enable him to pass two messages – one to the commentators and the other to the Press Liaison Steward. He can then pass the information on to the press in the way which is best on the day.

Recorders
The recording stewards may consist of a team of from two to six people depending on the size and complexity of the meeting. They should, ideally, be situated near the commentators and should receive a duplicate copy of track results sheets and be second in line to receive field-event cards. If match scores are involved one recorder should have as his sole task the keeping of a running score so that the commentators – and thus the spectators – are up to date on the match position. They should also keep any application-for-record forms and ensure, in the event of a record being set, that the form is completed *before the athletes and officials have left the stadium.*

Statistical co-ordinator
In important meetings it is essential for the commentators to have a back-up man whose only requirement is a deep knowledge of athletics

and particularly of the participants. It is virtually impossible for every commentator to know every possible piece of information about an event or a competitor and so a statistical co-ordinator (usually a member of the National Union of Track Statisticians) can be an important provider of further background information.

TECHNICAL OFFICIATING

The various technical duties are given in the IAAF Handbook and the handbooks of the various governing bodies. In addition most club meetings of note will have qualified officials anyway, well versed in their tasks. The uniniated are referred to the appropriate schools section, 'Organising a sports day'.

Officials must be treated well. They must be paid their expenses wherever possible and at least be given an adequate refreshment ticket at the conclusion of the meeting. In Britain we have the best and most enthusiastic technical officials in Europe and whether we keep in that happy position rests, in part, upon meeting organisers.

OTHER MEETING ADMINISTRATION

Apart from the technical officials other appointments must be made by the Officials Committee:

(1) Assistants to the clerk(s) of the course – for the very big meetings
(2) Competitors stewards
(3) Officials stewards

TRACK LIAISON

Make sure that the stadium manager, ground staff and other interested people have a timetable of events well in advance and know the exact requirements of the meeting.

SMALLER MEETINGS

For the smaller type of inter-club meeting the organisers will have much to do which will automatically occur with a bigger type of meeting. For instance, it is not always certain with such meetings if the Press intend to be present and it will be the task of the publicity committee (probably one man with a smaller meeting) to ensure that all is known and to link with the local sports editor to make sure what is required from the organisers. Basically though if the format indicated hitherto is followed, if only by a small team of organisers, with it appropriately scaled down, then the meeting should go well. It may well be that one man will take on more than one of the tasks. For the one-man organisation team the following check-list for the morning of his meeting might be useful:

(1) Arrive early in the day
(2) Inspect the track and field with the clerk of the course. Note any deficiencies and have them rectified immediately
(3) Double-check all necessary field event equipment including measuring tapes and have all deficiencies immediately rectified
(4) Have a young assistant along with you – perhaps a club junior – whom you can send hither and thither
(5) Re-check the list of required items and make sure that any deficiencies noted on the first check have been rectified
(6) Check the local weather forecast
(7) Check the refreshment arrangements
(8) Check with the public address firm that there will be no last-minute snags and that it will be arriving at the time previously specified
(9) Do everything possible to ensure a prompt start to the meeting
(10) Keep in touch with the arrival of officials and visiting teams and athletes, note any absentees and get ready to switch officials if problems arise
(11) Make sure that you have something to eat and drink at lunchtime
(12) Keep in touch with all events throughout the meeting. Keep on the move trying to forestall snags
(13) Keep cool
(14) Thank everybody at the end
(15) Relax and forget it all during the evening

POST-MEETING WORK

Letter of thanks
A brief, standard letter of thanks signed by the Meeting Director or the Chairman or Secretary of the host club should be sent to everyone who has assisted in any way at all within two weeks of the meeting.

Review meeting

Each Chairman of the twelve sub-committees should consult with his members to review how the meeting went, investigate the problems which arose, note the successful features and collate suggestions for smoother running or better presentation. These should be discussed in a complete review meeting of the Meeting Organisation Committee which should take place within *one month* of the date of the meeting. By this time all accounts should have been cleared and reactions gained from visiting clubs and athletes and the Press.

For the one-man organisation team a file for the running of next years meeting should be opened immediately with all relevant information included so that a fresh person could take over the running of the meeting without too many problems.

12

Public relations and Press publicity

These are so vital to the success of any club that they certainly deserve a special sub-committee in the scheme of team management. *Public relations* can be defined as the relations that the club has with the local community and if sufficiently large enough with the country's athletics' population as a whole. *Press publicity* can be defined as the best and easiest method – but not the only one – of doing this.

If the club is lucky enough to have a professional public relations man within its ranks it should do its best to coerce him into taking on the task on behalf of the club for he will already have a large number of contacts both locally and further afield. If they are not so fortunate, the ideal candidate will soon emerge, for public relations officers, whether professional or amateur, are not the most introverted of people. When appointed, there are a number of questions to which he must find the answers:

(1) Is the local town or community aware of the club's existence or success?

(2) Do the local Press have an 'athletics reporter'?

(3) Is contact made with the sports editors of the local Press?

(4) Has contact been made with the nearest local radio or TV station?

If the answers to any of these questions is no, then his first task is to remedy it straight away.

Local community awareness is vital for any club. From it stems so many things – spectators for home meetings, council aid and assistance, public support during appeals, etc. Regular news items and reports should appear in all the local papers and on the local radio, if there is one.

Any successes obtained must be pushed home to the full by arranging Press interviews with any champions and by supplying photographs of the club's top athletes. The important thing is to keep the information flowing.

PUBLIC RELATIONS

(1) Does the club bear the name of the local town or borough? This is becoming of increasing importance and should be seriously considered by any club committee

(2) Have personal contact with as many councillors and appropriate local government officers as is possible. Keep them informed of the club's activities – especially when the town's name is involved

(3) This can best be done by the publication, either monthly or quarterly, of a club magazine. Magazines can range from such examples as the Thames Valley Harriers' *The Interval* or Belgrave Harriers' *The Belgravian* to a simple duplicated sheet. Editing and producing (which means writing most of it as well) is a full-time job for anyone in the club

(4) It is often good public relations to have a local dignatory, such as the Mayor or Chairman of the Council as Club President

(5) If there is a local carnival or town show or sports festival, suggest that the club runs a meeting in conjunction with it

(6) Ask the local carnival or flower-show or rag-week Queen to present the prizes at one of your meetings

(7) Hold an annual dinner and dance and invite all the local council people who have either helped you or whom you think can help you, along as guests of honour

(8) Link up in some way with your local town football or rugby club – can you run a couple of races at half-time during one of the home matches?

(9) If you can afford it have posters made for your major home fixtures and ask shops in the town centre if they will display them

(10) Don't be frightened to use gimmickry: have the more glamorous women members and/or wives and girl friends handing out posters and leaflets in the town shopping centre on a Saturday morning

(11) Make sure that every local school is aware of your existence

and invite the physical education teachers and headmasters of the more athletically conscious as guests at your home fixtures

(12) Support local charities with collections at home meetings

(13) If there is a local rugby/football/speedway/greyhound stadium in action near the time of some of your meetings, ask for publicity to be put out over the public address system

PRESS PUBLICITY

(1) Have a Press Officer (can also be the Public Relations Officer)

(2) Make sure that he has a good link with the sports editors of the local newspapers and if there is an 'athletics correspondent' get to know him very well (take him out for a beer occasionally). Remember that you are part of his bread and butter

(3) If there is no local athletics correspondent, then the sports editor would most likely welcome you as the man/woman to do the job

(4) At the beginning of the track season and cross-country season give the local Press as much in-depth information as you can. Full fixture list; hopes for the club; outstanding prospects within the various teams. Supply photographs, if possible, of your best athletes

(5) Feed regularly (once a week) information, particularly stories, about athletes, e.g. CLUB HALF-MILE CHAMPIONS WED; STEEPLECHASE CHAMPION ATTACKED BY TERRIER IN CENTRAL PARK; LOCAL GIRL WINS COUNTY SCHOOLS TITLE. The local paper(s) may not use all that you send in, but it will be background information for which the correspondent/sports editor will be grateful

(6) Constantly strive to understand the *position* of newspapermen and assist them as much as possible

(7) Attempt to glamourise the sport for greater public appeal

(8) As big occasions approach (the club's big promotion or needle match), increase the flow of information to saturation

(9) Never give one newspaper 'exclusives'. Be equally fair to all Press and local radio

(10) Make sure that teams visiting your meeting send you full information concerning their teams and also telephone you up-to-date team news and 'stories'. Stress the need for the latter. JIM BLAKE BREAKS HONEYMOON TO RUN FOR EVESDALE

HARRIERS IN VITAL PROMOTION LEAGUE MATCH is much, much more newsworthy than JIM BLAKE RAN ONLY FOUR SECONDS OFF BEST TIME-TRIAL AT WEEK-END

(11) Make sure that you do the same when you are travelling to an inter-club or league meeting

(12) If you have an outstanding athlete, try to get him interviewed by Press and local radio before staging big meetings. The Press and the public like to equate meetings with athletes. People are more inclined to say 'I'm going to watch Dave Bedford run' than 'I'm going to the Southern Championships'

13
Links with outside authorities

For smooth and efficient administration and in order to take the fullest possible advantage of grants, amenities and other means of assistance, it is essential for a club to maintain good contact with authorities outside track and field. In dealing with such authorities the athletics club should endeavour to become one of the 'articulate minority' who, by dint of their contacts and knowledge, are able to deal more than successfully with the various bureaucratic machines. Outside bodies may be listed as follows: local authority, local education authority, and sports councils.

LOCAL AUTHORITY

Possibly the most contact will be with the local parks department and the appropriate council committee. This applies especially if the track and other facilities used are owned by the local authority. In this case regular and close contact with the local Director of Parks and his staff is of top priority. It must be remembered that athletics demands very sophisticated and complicated facilities and equipment and that no athletic club on its own can really justify the installation and maintainence of an athletics track. Incessant demands and numerous complaints are not the best way to obtain improvements, especially when a club has only fifty members.

A club should ascertain firstly who has control of the facilities that they use. In most cases it will be the local parks department, under whatever guise it is existing. Often there is a complicated administrative process with the maintainence of the track being carried out by the parks department and the actual hiring and running of the track being carried out by a separate recreation department. Many local authorities are inclining towards the appointment of Recreation Officers whose task it is to run and foster the whole field of sport in a certain district. Undoubtedly, with changes imminent in the early seventies in the pattern of local authority administration, this tendency will increase.

These changes in the pattern of local government should be noted carefully by club administrators for they will have a profound affect on the facilities that they use and in the type of grants that will be forthcoming. In general the pattern in 1974 will be towards larger units of local government which although, on the one hand, can mean a more remote administration can, on the other, mean more money being available for the improvement of established or the building of new facilities.

Many clubs have regular meetings with their local parks department and the most important are at the end of the track season which review possible improvements that could be made, discuss those facilities which need improving, especially where a safety factor is involved. The timing of this meeting is important and the club should ascertain when the department has to put in its estimates for the following financial year, which usually runs from April to March. In most cases such estimates must be made by the end of the year, so any representations for improvements should be made by November at the latest.

Good liaison must also extend to the actual ground staff of the facilities themselves, where friendly relationships are of great importance. The onus, as in most things, must be on the club, for it is in their interest to keep the groundsman happy. Help him in every way possible. Make sure that the equipment is always taken back, that changing rooms are left in a reasonable condition and that the junior section of the club does not rampage uncontrolled.

No groundsman is in the job because of the fantastic standard of living it gives him and many of them are dedicated men operating under severe handicaps. Some clubs appoint committees whose specific terms of reference are to liaise with the ground staff of the facilities that they use and with parks departments. Invite the groundsman to away-matches and to club social events. For the co-operative man, a good sized bonus at Christmas would certainly not go amiss and would help to cement relations. The more a club can make the groundsman feel part of them, the easier everyone's task will be. As in any walk of life there are good groundsmen and bad groundsmen: if you are lucky enough to have a good one, cultivate him as you would any asset;

if you have a bad one, do your best to educate him and if all else fails make representations to your Director of Parks.

Sometimes local authorities wish to run athletics meetings in conjunction with local sports weeks, carnivals or special occasions. They should turn to the local club for major assistance and may even ask it to run the whole thing. Such occasions should be seized with alacrity for it is a golden opportunity for the clubs to run a massive public relations exercise on its own behalf. In London, the Greater London Council Parks Department run the GLC Championships; in Mountain Ash the local authority give enormous support to the New Year races of Nos Galan. Other authorities run athletics meetings in conjunction with agricultural shows. Do not let the whole thing backfire because of abysmal organisation and presentation.

Finally, find out if the local authority give any grants to local clubs, either for improvement of facilities or the building of a club house. New policy emerging in the early seventies will incline towards encouraging local government grants in this field rather than grants from the national exchequer. Find out about such grants. Remember that local government is the servant of the local ratepaying public and don't ever, under any circumstances, feel or be intimidated by them. Take time over appointing a liaison officer. He must be one of the 'articulate minority' that seem, in these modern times, to be achieving more and more against bureaucracy; he must be patient, yet determined and well-versed in local government folklore.

LOCAL EDUCATION AUTHORITY

It will be very surprising if the athletic club does not need to have contact with the local education authority. Some tracks are run by the LEA, especially those connected with schools or colleges. The great majority of indoor training facilities which a club may need to use are in schools and colleges and the hire of these will be *via* the local education authority. *Unless the school is a private or direct-grant school, all enquiries and representations should be made to the local education officer.* This is very important. So often clubs make the initial contact with the headmaster or even the caretaker of a school or college, receive an initial rebuff and take the matter no further. In all instances deal with the local education authority. In rural areas this may well mean an approach to an authority some distance away. In nearly every instance the point of contact will be the Physical Education Organiser.

Every club should discover who the Physical Education Organiser for their particular area is, and institute a regular dialogue. He has contract with every school in his area and makes regular visits; he knows which schools actively encourage athletics; he knows about the availability of grants and how to qualify them and, finally, he can act as the 'trouble-shooter' between the club and the school. Establish and keep friendly contact, invite the organiser to club functions and to present the occasional trophy. Do not over-burden him with requests for he is often much over-burdened himself with a multitude of sports.

As with the groundsman, so with the school and college caretaker. It is in the club's interests to have a friendly and co-operative caretaker for the premises that you use. An evening's work usually means over-time and the man won't be too delighted with the extra quarter of an hour that you need in the weight-training room, the gymnasium or the showers, so don't ask for it. Make sure that you are finished and out of the building by the allotted time. The occasional gratuity in appreciation always goes down well.

Finally most youth service departments of an authority are within the education section. Find out who the local Youth Officer is and talk to him about the pros and cons of becoming an affiliated youth club. The minimum one can obtain by such affiliation is the hire of local facilities at a cheaper rate than the norm.

SPORTS COUNCILS

There are three types of Sports Councils (see Figure 11). Most liaison will be with the Local Sports Council, but initial enquiries are best made with the Regional Sports Councils. Local and Regional Sports Councils are advisory bodies, the former composed mainly of representatives of sports organisations and the latter mostly of representatives of local authorities who, in Britain, provide the majority of sports facilities. Sport is represented on the Regional Sports Councils by an allotted number of representatives of sport who come from a further body (in *most* areas!): Standing Conference of Sports Organisations. Each of the areas in Britain has its own individual policy but mainly speaking local clubs are represented on Local Sports Councils and County and Area Associations are represented on the Standing Conferences of Sport. All of these bodies deal mostly with the provision of facilities and the local athletic club should ensure that it is always represented at meetings.

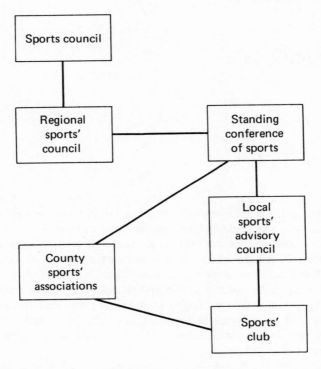

Figure 11

All information concerning sports councils in each area can be obtained from the appropriate Regional Sports Council (see *Appendix*) and any queries concerning grants, facilities or dissatisfaction with local handling of your problems should be made with the appropriate Regional Secretary. Even if he cannot handle your specific enquiry (and in the great majority of cases he will pass the matter on) he will be able to pinpoint immediately who to contact and will have noted what you have to say.

In Ireland a National Sports Council has recently been set up and certain monies are available from the national government though it seems likely for a while that such monies will go to the national associations of sport.

14

Facilities

This section is not intended as a comprehensive guide to the installation of full track and field facilities and any local authority or other organisation installing a track or other major facility is referred to the new joint AAA/NPFA publication which goes into the subject very thoroughly.

However, improvements and innovations are occuring so quickly in track and field that the administrative processes cannot keep up with them and, of necessity, handbooks and other publications are behind the times. In recent years three such innovations have rendered previous facilities obsolete: all-weather tracks, fibre-glass poles and the Fosbury style of high jumping.

Innovations will undoubtedly continue during the coming decade and the governing bodies, indeed the IAAF itself, should be setting up a think tank to try to forsee the changes and the actions that will be required. After all all-weather tracks are now installed throughout the world and are expected to last a minimum of fifteen to twenty years and perhaps very much longer, so designers should be thinking that far ahead attempting to assess track and field requirements for the 80s and 90s. Some likely innovations are:

(1) The growing introduction of synthetic grass in-fields. In the USA and Canada synthetic grass in-fields have already been introduced and at the present time this means that the long-throwing events of discus, hammer and javelin must take place outside the stadia. There are already such pitches installed in Britain, so some thought must be given to the provision of equipment for the long throws that can be used on synthetic in-fields

(2) World-records and consequent top-class international and national performances in the long throws will be too long for the present stadia. Either stadia must be larger – perhaps with the introduction of 500 metre tracks, which would be a much greater expense, or equipment must be made heavier. Certainly, thought should be given to the whole question of field equipment in view of improving records *and* synthetic grass. New styles and techniques could facilitate the situation

(3) Pole-vault performances will continue to improve with the concommitant requirements that landing areas will have to be larger and one can visualise huge landing areas of the order of 23–25 square feet being required

(4) The differential between international triple jumping and club and schools triple jumping will continue to widen, giving problems with the take-off points for this event, probably necessitating three or four separate boards

(5) Football and athletics stadia will be completely enclosed for major events. Some more accurate definition of an 'indoor record' will have to be formulated

Many other problems will undoubtedly occur and so one of the most important requirements for the seventies will be the setting up of a good communications system between those that govern and organise the sport and those that provide facilities for it. Local authority often has links with the local club, and some towns have a joint track committee composed of representatives of the local authority and those of the local club and other users – perhaps the District Schools Association.

When they are consulted by the local authority, the club will be asked primarily about design and lay-out, and, indeed, if they are asked deeper questions concerning engineering work for the track, they should refer the matter on to the National Association or the National Playing Fields Association. What follows is concerned primarily with the design and lay-out of facilities *as they stand at the beginning of 1973*. Clubs and committees are always looking for innovations and someone could, perhaps, be specifically appointed to carry out this task.

TRACKS

Cinder tracks should be of seven lanes or eight lanes. Where there are seven lanes, the inside one can be saved from excessive wear by using the outer six for appropriate events. Eight-lane tracks are usually of a national or regional significance and are rarely of cinder.

All-weather tracks should be of six lanes or eight lanes. The necessity for the seventh lane goes with new synthetic surfaces.

Design of tracks for the seventies should be such that those events which can be assisted or hindered by the wind can be run in either direction. This means (see Figure 12) allowing for sufficient run-in even if the 200 metres is run in a reverse direction. This will mean additional track markings.

FIELD EVENTS

The orientation of field-events must take into account a number of factors which are common to most of them:

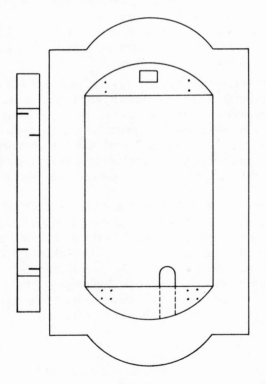

Figure 12

(1) Direction of the prevailing winds
(2) Siting of the track according to the position of the sun at the time that the event is likely to be held, e.g. vaulters must not vault into the sun
(3) Field-event facilities must be so placed that with a normal athletic programme they will not interfere with each other unduly

HIGH JUMP

With the new Fosbury technique and the introduction of portable landing areas the present high jump fan is now obsolete. Clearly, the use of sand pits must now be actively discouraged and the terminology is now 'landing area' rather than 'pit'. Ideally the whole of the semi-circle of the track should be used as a huge multi-purpose area for high jump and pole vault as at Mexico City and Helsinki in recent years. This can easily be done if portable landing areas are used (see Figure 10). There would in this instance be no set landing area. The advantages of a mobile area are obvious and could also take in the javelin approach area.

Types of landing area
Types of landing area vary. For the bigger stadium which hopes to stage some type of major meeting during the year, some expenditure on a sophisticated type of portable foam landing area is justified. At more minor tracks and schools one, of the smaller landing areas can be purchased or a do-it-yourself policy be pursued.

Two sizes of 'home-made' landing area can be made. The minimum is 10 feet × 5 feet × 1 foot 3 inches and for clubs 14 feet × 8 feet × 2 inches. Foam should be the main ingredient, bulked or made up (seat cushions are ideal), built on a frame and the whole covered by two canvas covers. Cost varies enormously, but should be between £16 and £30. Portable landing areas cost approximately £150.

POLE VAULTING

Landing areas
Much of what has been written about high jumping applies to pole vaulting – the essential of a landing area is that it must be soft (which means large quantities of foam) and must have no hard protruberances.

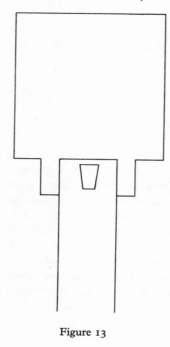

Figure 13

It is also important (see Figure 13) to have extensions to the landing area extending back along the sides of the runway in case the vaulter fails to make the vertical. When not in use, cover the area with a large tarpaulin.

For the large tracks more sophisticated portable landing areas are recommended, but these are expensive. Other tracks and schools can build their own areas and some study of the area at the Cavendish School, Hemel Hempstead may be useful. Landing areas should be a minimum 16 feet × 16 feet × 3 feet of foam in depth.

Runways

Avoid at all costs a cross-wind. Ideally, the use of the inside semi-circles of tracks is ideal for major pole-vaulting competitions, where two landing areas could be used to shorten the duration of them.

If a more conventional runway is used and has only one landing area, it is important that this goes with the prevailing wind. Figure 13 gives an idea of a dual pole vault area. Minimum length is 100 feet and the maximum about 140 feet.

Boxes

There are still many obsolete boxes in this country and it is important, in view of fibre-glass vaulting, that the box should have sloping sides and should be up against something solid.

Poles

We can do no better here than to quote direct from the article: 'Pole Vaulting for the Seventies', by Morton Evans, the BAAB National Event Coach for pole vault in the December 1971 issue of *Athletics Coach:*

Having provided a safe landing area it is now time to invest in poles. At the outset I must emphasise the importance of acquiring glass-fibre poles. Flexible poles are here to stay . . . bamboo poles (well maintained) can be very helpful. Every carpet delivered to a shop has a bamboo pole inside.

The most economical glass pole in the U.K. is the Bantex, developed by and marketed by Senior Coach Alan Neuff. This is ideal for beginners and quite economical. Similar poles from France are manufactured by. . . . High quality poles such as Catapole and Sky Poles are imported from the U.S.A. but are most costly because of import duty and freight charges.

Glass poles come in a very wide range of lengths and flexes. Each pole has a stress reference number which is often confusing, e.g. a 150 pole is, on average, supposedly intended for a vaulter weighing 150 lbs. However it varies according to height of handhold, combined with the amount of force applied on take-off. Thus it is possible for a vaulter to use several models as long as he varies his handhold and power of approach accordingly. The ideal collection of poles for a group of beginners would be 100, 110, 120 and 130 models. This would allow for progressions from pole to pole as the vaulter improves in different phases of the technique.

These poles must be looked after very carefully and used wisely. A pole generally breaks when a vaulter holds too high on a pole which is too 'floppy' for him. A glass pole should always be carried and bent in the same direction. This will condition the fibres to stretch consistently. Some form of indicator should be conspicuous on each pole e.g. a strip of tape along the section of the pole.

If only one or two poles can be bought by a school then the 110 and 120 should be bought and progress should be made on to the 130 etc.

Uprights and crossbars (also high jump)

For training, a length of ordinary white elastic, looped at each end and stretched between the uprights. These uprights must be very secure. For both vaulters and high jumpers the advantages are:

(1) Economy. Metal laths break very easily with soft landing areas
(2) Not painful
(3) Time saving. If the vaulter or jumper stretches the elastic down to the landing areas is swishes back up to the height and is then ready for the next athlete

In competition, some schools and clubs may find difficulty, as the landing areas get larger in spanning the gap with a cross-bar. In Figure 14 a simple pair of extensions is shown which can be easily made in a workshop and fixed to each upright.

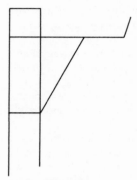

Figure 14

LONG JUMP AND TRIPLE JUMP

Standard runways are usually 4 feet to 4 feet 3 inches wide with about 140 feet of approach run in each case. All-weather facilities can reduce the width of the approach run to 2 feet 6 inches or 3 feet, but at the triple-jump board it is recommended that the width be widened to 4 feet, as the jumper can move from side to side as he is performing the three phases of the jump.

However, where large numbers of athletes, as in a school or a training college, are involved, the width of the runway could be increased to 16 feet with appropriate-sized pits.

In all cases, the runway should be a 'dual' one (see Figure 15) with a pit at each end. With a 180 feet length, both long and triple jumps can be accommodated together.

THROWING CIRCLES

Shot circles present little problem, except that the stop boards should be firm and the landing area should preferably be of cinder. Provision of discus and hammer circles presents a few more problems. Hammer throwers require a smooth surface on their circle, whilst discus throwers require a rougher grade of concrete. There is the added complication that discus throwers much prefer a contrary wind. This is probably best resolved by the placing of two circles diagonally opposite to each other in the centre of the track, one of rough texture facing the prevailing wind and one of smooth texture. Should the prevailing wind change, the discus thrower has the choice between a rough-surface circle or wind advantage. To avoid too many complicated markings, the areas should be marked with temporary tape for competitions. Cages will be required for both circles.

JAVELIN

Two javelin areas are also coming into vogue in major stadia. On all-weather surfaces, cost can be kept down by using the track itself as part of the runway and cutting the standard width down to between 6 feet and 8 feet.

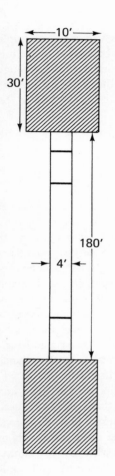

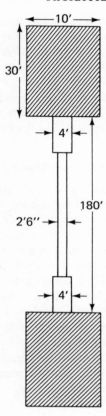

Figure 15

INDOOR FACILITIES

With indoor facilities for athletics in Britain we are still some way from the indoor training area at the INS at Vincennes near Paris. Recently indoor areas have been opened at the Crystal Palace National Recreation Centre and West London Stadium. Certainly the sport should work out the sort of use it can make of the large number of sports halls which are being built throughout the country. With

113

portable landing areas and throwing nets and the use of indoor implements a good deal of training and coaching can be carried out. Clubs must be prepared to re-think their ideas on using facilities, though. They must be ready to maximise the hour that they have booked in a hall or gymnasium, e.g. be warmed up before entering the area so that they can begin technique work straight away.

Most local sports centres have weight-lifting facilities and full and intelligent use should be made of these.

MULTI-PURPOSE AREAS

Most schools can design and build jumping areas in quite an enclosed space. In designing all-weather (sic) hockey areas and football pitches some thought should be given to summer use, and such areas can be turned, in the summer months, to running tracks, usually of 300 metres. By building large pits on the extremities of such areas, they can be used for long and triple jump training, teaching and competition. Portable landing areas mean that high jumping and pole vaulting can be included, and carefully sited throwing areas can turn the whole rectangle into a full track and field facility. Not only is this useful for schools but also for clubs in rural areas where the installation of a full-scale track and field facility cannot be justified. The finest examples of such areas are at the Orangefield School campus in Belfast.

What athletics must learn is that, as its facilities become more and more sophisticated, it must evolve ways in which they can also be used by other sports. In encouraging indoor athletic tracks it must encourage highly portable tracks which can fit into a number of halls throughout the country and which can be erected and dismantled in a few hours. By making its high-jump areas rectangular or by using the full semi-circle areas inside the bends games such as volley ball can be played on an all-weather surface. Innovators of the future must be looking towards the most flexible type of facility as is possible.

Appendix A
Club affiliations

Affiliated track and field clubs have:

	Direct representation	Representation at annual meetings	Votes at annual meetings
ENGLAND & WALES			
County/District AAA	YES/NO*	YES	YES
English Area AAAs	NO (Midlands–YES)	YES	YES
Welsh AAA		YES	YES
County/District WAAA	YES/NO*	YES	YES
English Area WAAAs	NO (Midlands–YES)	YES	YES
Welsh WAAA AAA	NO	YES**	YES**
WAAA	NO	YES**	YES**
SCOTLAND			
District AAA	NO	see***	see***
Scottish AAA	NO	YES	YES

Women's District AAA	NO	YES	YES
Scottish WAAA	NO	YES	YES

NORTHERN IRELAND

Northern Ireland AAA	YES	YES	YES
Northern Ireland WAAA	YES	YES	YES
BRITISH AMATEUR ATHLETIC BOARD	NO	YES	NO

*–varies in each county/district according to size and number of clubs

**–clubs affiliate to Area Association and not direct to the AAA/WAAA

***–in Scotland, District Committees are elected at annual general meeting of the Scottish AAA.

Appendix B
Contacts

CLUB MANAGEMENT write to:

Concerning	1st instance	2nd instance (if unsatisfactory or no reply.)	3rd instance (if unsatisfactory or no reply.)
Area Leagues (AAA)	Area AAA	National League AAA	
Championships (Men)	County AAA	Area AAA	AAA
Championships (Women)	County WAAA	Area WAAA	WAAA
Coaching (Men)	County/District AAA	Area AAA	BAAB
Coaching (Women)	County WAAA	Area WAAA	BAAB
Hiring a National Coach	Area AAA	BAAB	
Cross-country (Men)	County AAA	Area X-Country Associations	ECCU/Welsh CCU/ Scottish CCU
Facilities	Area AAA	AAA	NPFA
First Claim Status of Athletes (Men)	Area AAA	AAA	

First Claim Status of Athletes (Women)	Area WAAA	WAAA	
Five-Star Award Scheme	Area AAA	AAA	
Officials (Men)	County AAA	Area AAA	AAA
Officials (Women)	County WAAA	Area WAAA	WAAA
Official Publications	BAAB		
Race Walking	Area RWAs	RWA	
Schools Athletics	District Schools AA	County Schools AA	National Schools AA
Breach of AAA Laws or Rules for Competition	Area AAA	AAA	
Breach of WAAA Laws or Rules for Competition	Area WAAA	WAAA	
Cross-Country (Women) Race Walking (Women)	Area Womens Association*	Womens Association	

*–there is a combined association for women for Race Walking and Cross-Country.

Appendix C

Timetable of events for inter-club or inter-school match

1.00 pm	Hammer/Pole vault
2.00 pm	Long jump
2.15 pm	Discus/High jump
2.30 pm	400 metres hurdles
2.45 pm	800 metres
3.00 pm	100 metres
3.15 pm	3,000 metres steeplechase/triple jump
3.30 pm	110 metres hurdles
3.40 pm	Shot put/javelin
3.45 pm	400 metres
4.00 pm	1,500 metres
4.15 pm	200 metres
4.30 pm	5,000 metres
5.00 pm	4 × 100 metres relay
5.25 pm	4 × 400 metres relay

(The above timetable is for a National Athletics League match involving six clubs. Obviously it will need adapting for a girls' dual inter-school fixture etc. But the general pattern of the programme is a useful guide.)

Appendix D
Equipment/required items check-list

Application forms for records
Benches for competitors
Bell
Bouquet (for VIP wives etc.)
Chairs
Clip boards
Competitors' numbers
Copies of relevant rules for
    competition
Cross bars
Discoii
Duplicating equipment
Electronic loud-hailer
Extra events apparatus
Finishing posts
First Aid equipment
Fork-lift truck
Guest-seating lists
Hammers
High-jump stands
Hurdles and transporters
Javelin
Judges cards (track and field)
Judges stand
Lap scoring cards and numbers
Line-marking machine
Officials badges

Pole-vault stands
Press hut/area and telephones
Prize table
Public address system
Putting shots
Record indicator flags/markers
Recorder's forms, tables and
    tent/area
Refreshment arrangements
Relay batons and signal flags
Rope for field-event areas
Safety-pins
Spare shells, starting pistols,
    stop-watches
Shovels, forks and rakes
Starting blocks
Tape measure (one of
    100 metres)
Timekeeper's stand
Trolley for track-suits
Typewriters
Vaulting poles
Victory or award plinth
Whistles
Wind gauges
Wool

Training and Technique

I

Coaching

ORGANISATION OF COACHING

The organisation of coaching in Great Britain is based on a three-tier system consisting of a first, second and third tier, as follows:

First tier
Two principal National Coaches and the Coaching Administrator.

The two principal National Coaches are responsible for all technical development including the organisation of coaching for the national track and field teams and the overseeing of all groups of event specialisation.

Second tier
All National Coaches together with other senior coaches specifically nominated for event responsibility.

Their duties are concerned with event specialisation and responsibility at all national levels and also with the development of selected top-class athletes in the events for which they are responsible. National Coaches also have regional and area responsibilities.

Third tier
All senior coaches, club coaches, assistant club coaches and teachers holding the appropriate qualification. Their duties include coaching or assisting with coaching at area, region, county, club and school level.

Within the senior coach structure, appointments have been made to staff coach. Such appointments are made by areas or regions in consultation with the national and event coaches. Staff coaches have an important role in the event responsibility aspect of the scheme.

Any young athlete who requires coaching would be advised to contact the coaching department of his area or national organisation and they will be able to put him in touch with the coach who lives nearest to his home.

THE COACHING SESSION

Coach and athlete should meet either once or twice a week. On one of these occasions the coach will be involved in actively coaching the athlete and on the other he may just watch him in training. A club coach has to divide his time among a number of athletes and it is not always possible to coach every athlete at each club practice.

The session can begin with a mass warm-up at the track for all the athletes and this can be taken by the club coach with assistant coaches to help him. It will begin with jogging, running and suppling exercises, followed by striding and some sharper bursts over about 80 metres. The track suit should be worn in cold weather for all this preliminary work and taken off only when the more technical work begins.

The club coach should come to the track with a clear plan in his mind for all the events under his control. His assistants can each be given groups to help or supervise by timing, measuring or recording. In some cases they will be coaching specific skills under the direction of the coach. Some clubs may be fortunate and have several coaches capable of looking after events to a higher level. In this case, each one could be given a specific group of events to look after for the season, e.g. jumping, sprinting, hurdling, throwing, etc. Assistant coaches can often be recruited from amongst the mothers and fathers who come to the track to watch their youngsters perform. An enquiry by the club coach may unearth a father or mother who was at one time a good performer and who still knows something about one or two events. In this case they should be encouraged to take up coaching at the club. The club coach and club secretary can do a lot to persuade these people to give a hand rather than sit in their cars waiting for the session to end.

WAYS IN WHICH THE COACH CAN HELP THE ATHLETE LEARN TECHNIQUES AND TECHNICAL SKILLS

By personal demonstration
If the coach happens to be a good demonstrator then this can be useful.

However, if the coach is young enough to demonstrate well, he is seldom old enough to have experience.

Getting an expert to demonstrate the event
This can be extremely valuable if the coach can talk about the event and outline the technique which is being shown by the demonstrator. This also has an inspirational value which has a big part to play in the early instruction of the young athlete.

Putting athlete in position and guiding
This is all right in the beginning because it gives the athlete some idea. However, all movements are performed at speed and, therefore, this method has its limitations.

Verbal instruction
The coach must spend a certain amount of time on each session instructing the athlete verbally. There are, however, certain pitfalls into which the coach can be drawn, even with the best of intentions, therefore:

(1) What he says must be brief and to the point. Coaches tend, by the nature of their profession, to become verbose. Too much instruction is both tedious and confusing to the athlete. It is far better to say too little than too much because the short sharp instruction will at least be put into effect because it will be heard and understood

(2) In cold weather, outdoor instructions should be given 'on the move'. Run with the athlete as he jogs back up the runway and tell him quickly what happened and how to correct the fault. In all cases be quick and decisive; do not come back and have second thoughts, explaining all over again something which you are not sure about

Asking the athlete to report back his sensations after each jump or throw
For instance, if the athlete has just cleared the bar with a 'Fosbury Flop' ask him to explain his sensations during the run-up, take-off and clearance. It is better to be specific and say something like, 'Where were your hips in relation to the rest of your body as you crossed the bar?' After the athlete has explained briefly to the coach what he thought happened, he may be surprised to be told by the coach that his sensations were wrong. The athlete must then go back and try

again until he gets the feeling the coach requires. This is an important aspect of coaching and in this way the coach also *learns* and builds up a mental picture of what it feels like to the athlete.

Getting the athlete to explain the technique of his event to others

In the club hut during the winter months this can be an interesting and profitable exercise. Also, on the track, an experienced athlete can sometimes help the coach instruct beginners because he has had the feeling of certain situations himself. The coach cannot have experienced every event himself to high level and, therefore, the experienced athlete can be of assistance to him at certain times.

Mental practice

The coach should give the athlete a true picture of the event and the sensations experienced on each successive movement. He should then ask the athlete to go through the whole skill over and over again in his mind. This form of mental training has been shown to produce an immediate improvement in performance.

Cine film

This is a first rate method of instruction. Take film of the athlete both in competition and training and show it to him many times with comments and criticisms. Let him sit down by himself, watching it and comparing it with champions in the same event. All the time he will be learning.

Video tape

This is better than cine film in that the athlete performs his event in training and can then walk straight across and see exactly what he has done. His sensations are still with him as he watches his every movement on the television screen. Although this is the ultimate in training aids, it is inevitably very expensive to hire.

Drawings, photographs, strip pictures and technical articles

These are ideal for the club coach – easy to obtain and inexpensive. They should be pinned round the walls of the club hut both for their instructional and inspirational value. Young boys and girls should be encouraged to read about top athletes, get to know what they look like and how they perform and train. The club should buy suitable magazines and make them available to club members.

THE COACH ATHLETE RELATIONSHIP

The first requisite of the coach is that he should be available. The athlete should be able to see him at least once a week at the track and he should be available for advice at other times. The coach must also be on time; if the athlete knows the coach will be on time, there is far less likelihood of him cutting a session or being late. The coach must be the driving force behind the athlete and the onus must always fall on him.

The coach must have sufficient technical knowledge to teach the athlete the fundamentals of his event. He must also be capable of imparting this knowledge to the athlete in terms that he can understand and interpret into physical movement. Many people can learn and understand the technical skills underlying an event, but not so many can 'get it over' in a way which will get results. It is only by experience that the coach can understand the feelings of the athlete on the end of a pole and formulate phrases which mean anything to a boy in this situation. Hence it is essential that the coach gets experience by coaching and not just by reading technical books. Reading is important but it is more important to see and appreciate physical movement.

BASIC EQUIPMENT FOR THE CLUB COACH

Clip board with pencil attached, preferably with waterproof cover and
    metal clip to hold a watch
First aid kit (small)
10 metre tape measure
One pair of flat training shoes
Pair of pliers for removing spikes
Pair of wooden clappers to use instead of a starting pistol
Penknife
Safety pins (various sizes)
Scissors
Short steel tape measure for block spacing and stride length measure-
    ments
Spare shoelaces
Starting pistol and ammunition
Stop watch
Talcum powder, useful for shoes and checkmarks
Whistle

Stop watches vary – for sprinting, a 10-second dial sweep with a split hand is preferable. For middle distance, a 60-second sweep measured in 10ths, with a split hand for lap times, is essential. The coach should remember that he will be standing out in all weathers, so warm waterproof clothing and footwear is necessary throughout the winter and spring. Remember, also, that the head needs protection when one is standing still in cold winds for several hours; the waterproof jacket should also have a hood to cover the head.

2

Sprinting

Sprinting is running at or close to maximum speed. An athlete may hold top speed for a little while, a very fit athlete may hold top speed for longer. In the 100 metres there is very little falling off from top speed and it may be described as a pure sprint. The 200 metres is close to being a pure sprint but the runner does not attempt to hold full speed throughout the race. The novice should use a fast start, a period of coasting round the turn followed by a full-effort burst down the home straight. The next stage is to use a fast start and merely drop tension round the bend sufficiently to enable the athlete to hold close to a maximum speed to the finish. The 400 metres, although run at a slower speed than either the 100 or 200 metres, is still classified as a sprint: it is a sustained sprint in which the first 200 metres is generally run one or two seconds faster than the second 200 metres.

Sprinting is a combination of leg speed and stride length. Improvement is brought about by increasing stride length through extra mobility and strength. This is done during the winter months by carrying out a progressive strength-training programme with weights alongside a carefully planned set of mobility exercises. Greater leg speed can only be obtained by improvement in technique and better co-ordination of the limb movements. Hence technique work does play an important part in a sprinter's training both in and out of season.

COACHING (see figure on p. 202)

As far as technique is concerned, the coach should concentrate on the starting position, movement away from the blocks during the pick-up period of the race, body carriage and limb movements, the ability of the athlete to open out into full stride quickly and the finish.

However, as with all running events, the coach must attend to the proper conditioning of his charges. With each race, from 100 metres upwards to Marathon, accepted training practices vary according to the physiological requirements of the athlete over any given distance. Obviously, the main requirements of the 100 metres sprinter will be strength and mobility but, as the distance get longer, the endurance factor will become more and more important.

Coaching position (1) to the side, 10–20 metres from the athlete
Starting position
(1) Hips in line or slightly higher than the shoulders
(2) Shoulders in advance of the starting line
(3) Straight back
(4) Angle at front knee 90 degrees
(5) Angle at rear knee 120 degrees
(6) Front block 15–19 inches behind the line but this will vary with the individual
(7) Distance between blocks from front to rear generally varies from 12–20 inches. The tendency at the present time is for the spacing to be not so great, in the case of many top class sprinters, 12 inches or less
(8) It is better for the shoulders to be forward in the 'on your marks' position, then when the command 'set' is given all the athlete has to do is raise the hips

Coaching position (2) front
(1) Arms straight
(2) Hands placed shoulder-width apart
(3) Up on the fingertips with as high a bridge as possible of forefinger and thumb
(4) Hands equidistant from the centre bar of the blocks. This can be checked by scratching a line on the ground

Coaching position (3) rear
(1) Heels vertical
(2) Knees and feet in line
(3) A gap of about 2 inches between the knees
(4) In the 200 metres the blocks are placed on the outside of the

lane and angled inwards so the sprinter can run straight for the first few yards of the race

TRAINING

All training is a highly individual matter and no schedule should be set without full knowledge of the athlete, the environment and the facilities that are available. However, some guidance can be given to the coach and the following is a general outline of the type of work which can be given to senior boys and girls. The sessions are merely listed; their selection each week and order of presentation to the athlete can only be arranged by the man on the spot, or the athlete if there is no coach available. The coach should remember that there is basically very little difference between a man and a woman when it comes to training for athletics. The type of work applies equally to boys and girls and it is only in the modification of the sessions to allow for a girl having less strength and endurance than a man that the coach must be careful. For instance, weight training should be started gradually with a girl, and, in all probability, it will be more convenient to initiate girls into a progressive resistance programme by using the body weight and portable apparatus rather than bars and iron discs.

100 metres and 200 metres winter
(1) *Fartlek* (3–5 miles) Fast stretches interspersed with steady running and slow recovery jogs. This session should be carried out on grass if possible but if this is impossible, it may be necessary to use the roads because they are lighted. The fast stretches should vary from 60 metres–200 metres
(2) *Hill running* Repetition runs up short, steep slopes with a slow jog to recover
(3) *Weight training or progressive resistance exercise* One or other, or a mixture, should be carried out on three days per week with a day's rest in between. Although the emphasis for runners should be on the upper body, which is generally under-developed in comparison to the lower parts, the legs should not be neglected. Step-ups, straddle lifts and squats should also be in the sprinter's schedule. Harness running also falls into this category and this is also a useful practice technique for the beginner. The arm action, drive and knee-lift can be emphasised

(4) *Circuit training* can be a useful adjunct to a sprinter's training throughout the winter. However, providing the sprinter is doing weight-training plus other endurance work on the hills and on the track, there is little point in a session of this type. There is more case for the 400 metres runner doing circuit training two or three times a week because he must have greater powers of endurance

(5) *Typical track workouts in winter*
  (a) 6 × 300 metres (5 minutes recovery)
  (b) 4 × 150 metres (2½ minutes rest)
      7 minutes rest
      4 × 150 metres (2½ minutes rest)
      10 minutes rest
      4 × 150 metres (2½ minutes recovery)
  (c) 12 × 60 metres (full effort) from blocks with a walk back recovery
  (d) 6 × 200 metres (¾ effort) 3½ minutes jog recovery
      10 minutes rest
      2 × 200 metres (full effort) 5 minutes recovery

All the runs should be at a pace which will allow the athlete to complete the session. However, a fast average rate should be maintained. There will be a big difference between the speed of boys and girls. For instance a girl might average 46–48 seconds for 6 × 300 whereas a boy will do them comfortably in 42–44 seconds. These times will obviously vary with the state of fitness, condition of the track and ability of the individual.

100 metres and 200 metres summer
  (1) 1 × 300 metres (full effort)
      10 minutes rest
      6 × 80 metres (full effort from blocks) 3½ minutes rest
  (2) 5 × 150 metres (full effort round bend) 5 minutes recovery
      10 minutes rest
      5 × 150 metres (full effort round bend) 5 minutes recovery
  (3) 6 × 60 metres (from blocks full effort) walk back recovery
      5 minutes rest
      6 × 60 metres (from blocks full effort) walk back recovery
  (4) Starting practice over 50 metres from blocks. A starting pistol should be used on this session and it should preferably be done

with other sprinters of an equal standard. Emphasis should be placed on simulating competition conditions. It is better to have finishing posts and a tape at the 50 metres mark, then the finish can be practised at the same time.

(5) 3 × 300 metres (full effort)
7 minutes recovery

(6) 1 × 150 metres (full effort from blocks)
5 minutes recovery
2 × 80 metres (full effort from blocks) 3½ minutes recovery
5 minutes recovery
4 × 60 metres (full effort from blocks) walk back recovery

The 200 metres runner must do a large proportion of his starts from the 200 metres start on the bend. It is also advisable for him to vary the lane in which he runs.

400 metres winter
The sessions of fartlek, hill running, weight training and circuit training apply equally to 400 metre runners. In fact the endurance factor is greater in the 400 metres so extra emphasis should be placed on the severity of the fartlek and hill-running workouts.

TYPICAL TRACK WORKOUTS

(1) *6 × 200 metres* (at racing speed, e.g. a 54-second 400 metres runner would run them in 26–27 seconds) 3½ minutes jog recovery

(2) *Differential 400 metres*
4 × 400 (200 slow – 200 metres fast) 5 minutes recovery
The last 200 metres should be run at racing speed for the distance, e.g. a 54-seconds 400 metres runner would run the first 200 metres in 32 seconds and the second 200 metres in 28 seconds. A girl should run the first 200 metres considerably slower, in 34–36 seconds. This is the reverse of the actual race, when the athlete would probably run 26 seconds and 28 seconds

(3) *10 × 150 metres* (full effort) 90 seconds recovery

(4) *Up-the-clock*
Starting with 120 metres and increasing the distance on each run by 10 metres until 200 metres is reached. All runs should be at maximum effort with the recovery periods starting at 2 minutes and increasing by half a minute every two runs. This session can be varied to suit the athlete

(5) *Differential 500 metres*
3 × 500 metres (300 metres slow – 200 metres fast) 7 minutes recovery, e.g. 300 metres – 50 seconds, 200 metres – 28 seconds

(6) *8 × 80 metres* (full effort round turn from blocks on bend) 3½ minutes recovery. Vary the lanes

Summer

(1) *4 × 200 metres* (maximum effort) 5 minutes recovery. 25 seconds for a 54-second 400 metres runner

(2) *6 × 150 metres* (full effort from blocks on the bend)

(3) *1 × 500 metres* (full effort)
10 minutes recovery
6 × 80 metres (full effort from blocks) 3½ minutes recovery

(4) *Up-the-clock*
As in session (4) winter schedule. Increase repetitions as fitness improves

(5) *Differential 400 metres*
3 × 400 metres (200 metres slow – 200 metres fast) 5 minutes recovery
First 200 metres (32) second 200 metres (26)

(6) Starting practice with the gun over 50 metres
10 minutes rest
2 × 150 metres (full effort from a rolling start)

3

Relay racing

The essential rules of relay racing are given in the IAAF Handbook, as rule 166:

1.—Chalk lines shall be drawn across the track to mark the distances of the stages and to denote the scratch line.

2.—Chalk lines also shall be drawn 10 metres (11 yards) before and after the scratch line to denote the take-over zone within which lines the baton must be passed. These lines are to be included in the zonal measurements. In races up to 4 × 220 yards (4 × 200 metres) members of a team other than the first runner may commence running not more than 10 metres (11 yards) outside the take-over zone. A distinctive mark shall be made in each lane to denote this extended limit.

In all relay races the baton must be passed within the take-over zone.

When a relay race is being run in lanes, a competitor may make a check-mark on the track within his own lane, e.g. by scratching with his shoe, but may not place marking objects on or alongside the track. Where the track is of a material which will not permit scratching with a shoe, some adhesive paper or powder may be used, at the discretion of the judge.

3.—The baton must be carried in the hand throughout the race. If dropped, it must be recovered by the athlete who dropped it.

4.—The position of the teams at the start of the race shall be drawn, and shall be retained at each take over zone, except that waiting runners can move to the inside position on the track as incoming team-mates arrive, provided this can be done without fouling.

5.—In events where the first part of the race is run in lanes, competitors, after completing this part, are free to take up any position on the track.

6.—Competitors after handing over the baton should remain in their lanes or zones until the course is clear, to avoid obstruction to other competitors. Should any competitor wilfully impede a member of another team by running out of position or lane at the finish of the stage, he is liable to cause disqualification of his own team.

4 × 100 METRES RELAY

As may be seen from the rules, each of the three baton changes must be made within a 20 metre zone. However, the outgoing runner may use an additional 10 metre zone to work up speed before entering the 20 metre exchange zone or box. In effect this means that, although the change must be made within the 20 metre zone the outgoing runner has 30 metres in which he may work up speed before receiving the baton.

There are two main factors in relay racing – sprinting speed and effective baton passing.

Both of these factors are vital to a good relay team. However, baton passing can be improved quickly, and to such an extent that it can make all the difference between a first-class relay team and a mediocre one. Therefore, nearly all the coach's time will be devoted to improving the speed of the baton around the track by every means at his disposal.

Having picked the relay team early in the season, the first thing to be decided is the best order of running. Here, there are several factors to be taken into consideration:

(1) The distance to be run with and without the baton on each leg. The following table is taken from *Track Athletics*:*

On the assumption that the changes will be affected 2 metres beyond the middle of the boxes each runner would cover the following approximate distances:

	Total distance run	Distance run with baton
1st runner	101.5 metres	101.5 metres
2nd runner	121.5 metres	99.0 metres
3rd runner	121.5 metres	99.0 metres
4th runner	120 metres	97.5 metres
		397.0 metres

The other 3 metres are covered by free distance, i.e. 1 metre at each change.

*By Bill Marlow and Denis Watts, published by Pelham Books.

(2) The first and third legs of the race are run mainly on the turns and, therefore, good bend runners are required on these stages

(3) The middle two runners must be able to receive and pass the baton well. They should also be the best runners over 121 metres which may mean that they are recruited from the 200 metres specialists

(4) The last runner will be running 120 metres down the straight. He should also be a good fighter and capable of receiving the baton in the left hand

METHODS OF BATON PASSING

All sprint relay techniques should be non-visual. In other words, once the incoming runner has reached the check mark, the outgoing runner commences to run at full effort and does not look round. After a given number of strides or as the centre line of the zone is passed the hand is placed back in a position from which the baton can be received.

Most relay teams use the alternate pass where the first and third runners carry the baton in the right hand and second and fourth runners use the left hand. This is because the first and third legs are round bends and by carrying the baton in their right hands the runners may hug the inside of the lane all the way round. The second and fourth runners will be on the outside of the lane for the duration of their run, which in both cases is mainly down the straight.

There are two basic methods for transferring the baton from one runner to the next – the down-pass and the upward-pass.

Both these methods have advantages and disadvantages which the coach should study before deciding to use one method or the other. The majority of national teams have rejected the down-pass because of the risks involved.

Down-pass
Advantages:
(1) The reach-back of the outgoing runner and reach forward of the incoming runner gives a little extra 'free distance' on each change
(2) As the runner receives the baton into an upturned palm there will be more of the baton forward ready for the next pass

Disadvantages:

(1) This method is very exacting in terms of practice. It is difficult for the outgoing runner to hold the hand flat and high behind and keep the hand steady when running at great speed. This problem has been accentuated since the introduction of the extra 10 metres acceleration zone giving extra speed to the outgoing runner

(2) If the incoming runner overshoots his partner it is very difficult to retrieve the situation

(3) Even with teams who have had great success with this method, it is very seldom, if ever, that three perfect changes have been seen in any one race

Up-pass

Advantages:

(1) It is very much safer than the down-pass. If either runner makes a slight error of judgement in either the approach or get-away, the situation can be retrieved with very little loss of baton speed

(2) It is not so exacting in terms of practice

(3) The outgoing runner can move off fast and still present a good hand to the incoming runner without much difficulty

Disadvantages:

(1) There is not so much 'free distance', i.e. distance which nobody runs, on each change. This is because the outgoing runner cannot reach so far back while presenting a flat palm inclined downwards towards the ground.

(2) Free distance is also lost because the incoming runner has to get as much of the baton forward into the outgoing runner's hand as possible. This is to give him as much of the baton in front of his hand as possible in order to facilitate the next change

ESTABLISHMENT OF THE CHECK MARK (see figure on pp. 204–5)

Initially this can be made approximately seven walking paces back from the beginning of the accelerating zone. If it is a cinder track, the mark is generally scratched or talcum powder is spread on the track surface. If, however, it is a synthetic surface, coloured adhesive should be used. This mark should be adjusted by practice between the two runners. The final measurement is made in foot lengths by placing the heel of one foot against the toes of the other. The total distance measured in this way generally works out between 26–34 foot lengths.

The method of changing the baton shown in the diagrams is the alternating up-sweep as used by most of the national teams in the world at the present time. Although it should be remembered that much of what is described under 'coaching positions' can, by adaptation, be applied to any method of change, certain fundamentals of technique being common to all methods.

COACHING POSITIONS

The main coaching position is 20 metres back and to the side of the estimated point of exchange. The coach must ensure that he is on the correct side of the runners so that he is in position to see the baton passed. Another observer may stand directly opposite the check mark to see that the outgoing runner moves off at the exact moment when the incoming runner is directly over the mark.

Common faults

(*1*) *Outgoing runner overtaken or caught too soon*
Correction
(1) Check with the observer, who was watching the check mark, that the outgoing runner left on time and not too late
(2) Ensure that the outgoing runner is driving out powerfully with legs and arms
(3) Ensure that the outgoing runner's turn and start are simultaneous
(4) If points (1), (2) and (3) are all right then adjust the check mark

Incoming runner failing to catch the outgoing runner, or outgoing runner
(*2*) *having to slow down to receive the baton within the zone*
Correction
(1) Check with observer that the outgoing runner did not go too soon
(2) Ensure that the incoming runner is coming in really hard and not fading at the end of the leg
(3) If points (1) and (2) are all right then adjust check mark

(*3*) *Outgoing runner failing to present a good hand for the incoming runner*
Correction
(1) Make the runner present a good hand in a stationary position.

137

Ensure the athlete feels the position with the elbow slightly bent and palm down (Figure a)

(2) Practise runs with one runner coming in to activate several runners. The hand should be presented some 15 metres from the start of the run and held momentarily in the correct position

4 × 400 METRES RELAY

The 4 × 400 metre relay has increased in popularity in recent years and has, since 1969, been an official event for women. Whereas brilliant baton passing is not as important as in the sprint relay, it is nevertheless a significant factor in the ultimate success of a relay team. It is, therefore, recommended that teams devote just as much time to practice as they can manage.

The change generally used is a non-visual change from the right hand of the incoming runner to the left hand of the outgoing runner. The change is an upward pass into the 'V' formed by the thumb and forefinger. The outgoing runner changes the baton from left hand to right hand immediately he has received it. The reason for receiving the baton in the left hand is that the outgoing runner, who will be entering the bend as he moves off, will be able to see the edge of the track and more easily negotiate the bend.

A check mark at about five metres is a useful guide to the outgoing runner. However, since the incoming runner is tiring, he must estimate the speed of his getaway accordingly. The responsibility of the change must be placed squarely on the shoulders of the outgoing runner who is fresh and able to make the necessary quick decisions. When eight runners are all coming in together, having broken from their lanes for the second and third changes, the outgoing runner must quickly estimate the position and speed of his incoming partner. This may mean he has to change position amongst the jostling of the other competitors.

The first leg of the race is run in lanes and so is the first bend of the second leg. This means that the first runner will be running 400 metres on a stagger for 500 metres. It is, therefore, important that the first runner be experienced and have good pace judgement. The last runner must be a better-than-average performer with good pace judgement and tactical sense. A weaker man, who will fight if 'pulled through' by an opponent who leads, would usually be placed as number 2 or number 3 runner in the team.

4
Middle distance running

GENERAL (see figure on p. 206)

The pure middle distance events are the 800 metres, the 1,500 metres and the 5,000 metres; the 10,000 metres is an intermediary race between middle and long distance.

In running both middle and long distances, the problems of the coach and athlete are more concerned with conditioning and less with technical considerations such as running style. The prime concern of the middle distance coach is the mental and physical preparation of his charges for competition. Most coaches find that their most exacting and difficult task is to find the right sort of competition at the right time in order to prepare the athlete for a major championship such as the Olympic Games.

The running action
There is little point in attempting to break down individual running 'style'. This is something which has been developed since childhood. The runner, over the years, has modified and corrected limb movements instinctively to suit his or her physical characteristics. However, in all types of running there is a basic pattern which should be followed in broad outline.

Arm action
In distance running the arms are used merely to balance the leg action. They should swing easily to the centre line of the body with an angle of approximately 90 degrees between the upper and lower arm. However, there will very often be an opening out and closing of the arm as it

swings. Provided this independent movement of the lower arm is not too exaggerated, and it balances the leg action, it should be left alone. Obviously the arms will be used more vigorously in an 800 metres race than in the 5,000 metres upwards.

Leg action

The cadence of the leg action is slower than that of sprinting and the knee lift is not so high. The runner is concerned with relaxation and economy of effort rather than stride length or rate of leg movements. The important fundamentals of a good leg action are a relaxed free movement of the legs and the maintenance of sufficient range of movement from the hips.

Body lean

This aspect generally takes care of itself. However, it will be less than in sprinting and will adjust itself according to the details of the runner's physique. The coach will soon see if the athlete is carrying his body awkwardly; there should be no interference with the smooth flow of the athlete's natural running action.

Tactical considerations

Once the runner has become racing fit his main consideration is to run, on each occasion, the best race of which he is capable. This to some extent depends on his mental state. He must go to the start of each race with a confident, aggressive attitude, keen to race and eager to succeed. This may well mean that the coach must limit the number of races run by the athlete; the natural tendency is to over-race. Competition, therefore, must be carefully planned well in advance and blend correctly with the conditioning of the runner and his state of fitness at any given time.

Tactical problems

Pace judgement should be one of the first considerations of the young runner. The coach should develop a good sense of pace in his charges at an early age. Lapping at racing speed with the use of a stop watch and whistle must play an important part in the training of any young middle distance runner. As the years go by, the athlete will develop a sense of pace and be able to estimate the speed at which he is running at any stage of the race.

There are certain golden rules in racing, such as:

(1) Keep in touch with the leaders preferably in second or third place and watch carefully to see that nobody decides to make a sudden break and open up a gap which cannot be closed.

(2) Avoid unnecessary changing of pace or position and try to run the middle part of the race as evenly as possible

(3) Avoid being boxed in, especially during the later stages of the race. In this respect it is always better to run off the shoulder of the runner immediately in front of you. This means you are in a position to respond at once to any tactical changes in the race

TRAINING

The methods of training in general use today are well known, but to lay down exactly how they should be apportioned to any given distance is impossible. Training is an individual matter and it depends on such vital factors as:

(1) The distance the athlete is training for, either 800 metres–1,500 metres which are anaerobic in nature or 5,000 metres–10,000 metres which are aerobic. In anaerobic running the O_2 intake at tissue level is not sufficient to balance the work which is being done – hence the athlete has to take up an oxygen debt. This is comparable to team games such as football and rugby where the player is running very fast for short periods and getting insufficient recovery before having to repeat the next fast run. In aerobic running the athlete is running more slowly and in a steady state. The proportion of anaerobic to aerobic running for any given distance is shown on the following standard table:

Event	Anaerobic	Aerobic
800m	67%	33%
1,500m	50%	50%
5,000m	80%	20%
10,000m	90%	10%
Marathon	99%	1%

This table shows that 800 metres/1,500 metres races are anaerobic in nature and, therefore, require mainly speed/endurance training and not so much interval running. They are high oxygen debt races.

5,000 metre/10,000 metre races are aerobic in nature and, therefore, interval running is more favourable. The expansion stimulus on the heart cavities eventually brings about adaption and the heart is enabled to pump more blood to the working muscles. This is a favourable factor in distance running

(2) *Environment and the facilities at the disposal of the athlete* The bias towards either one method of training or another will often be decided by the athlete's surroundings. If living in the open country without a track available, then the bulk of the training will be done in the form of fartlek, hill running and forms of interval running on level fields. If the runner is situated in an industrial area with a floodlit track open on, say, Tuesdays and Thursdays, then most of the steady distance running will have to be done on the roads or, if possible, along the grass verge of a highway. The runner should avoid the roads if possible but sometimes there is no other alternative. Interval running and speed/endurance work can be done on the nights when the track is floodlit and at week-ends

(3) The coach must also take into account the athlete's own individual inclination and preference for one method or another. All training must be enjoyable and it would be folly to force a young distance runner to carry out sessions of interval running which might involve 20 × 200 metres when he gets bored and fed up with the monotony of the work. In this case fartlek and running over open country would be far more beneficial. However, this is not to say that the coach must give in to the athlete's every whim. There are certain methods of training and they must be used intelligently and to the benefit of the individual

Cross country

The benefits of cross-country are many but it also has disadvantages for the track specialist. The distance runner can put in his essential mileage in an enjoyable and interesting manner. It keeps alive his competitive spirit and interest throughout the long winter and mileage is always 'money in the Bank' for any middle or long distance athlete. However, these advantages must be balanced against the fact that the runner is continually interrupting his training for competition throughout the year. The last two days of each week are geared to prepare for the competition on the following Saturday. Another clear disadvantage is that when a major track competition such as the Commonwealth

Games or European Championships is scheduled late in the year the British distance runner will have been competing from January until August–October.

Hill running

A certain amount of hill running can be extremely effective in building strength and endurance for all distances from 100 metres upwards. But again the emphasis on this type of work depends on the physical characteristics of the athlete and the distance he is running. As a general rule not more than two sessions should be done in each week and not on consecutive days.

Fartlek or speed play

Walking, running and jogging over open country as the mood of the runner dictates. This is not necessarily a training of the will but rather a hard and enjoyable outing sometimes through woods or along the seashore. Unless the athlete has a definite circuit to follow, the dose is generally administered on a time basis, such as *Fartlek – 1 hour*, with a short description of the type of work which is envisaged by the coach.

Long runs over 10–20 miles or Long, slow distance running

Most suitable for the distance runner but also to a lesser extent for the middle distance runner who wishes to improve capillarisation of the working muscles. Endurance gained from this method lasts longer than from any other type of training.

Interval running

This is a regimented method where the athlete runs a prescribed distance in a given time with a set recovery period on the track. The coach or athlete has several variables to play with in order to bring about the desired effect. For instance, he has the distance of the fast run, the time of the fast run, the number of repetitions of the fast run and the recovery period between the runs. A normal interval running session might consist of 20 × 200 metres (32 seconds) with 90 seconds recovery. The training effect comes at the end of the fast run when the heart fills rapidly during the next 30 seconds. This expansion stimulus lasts about 30 seconds and then dies away. Through many repetitions of this exercise the heart cavities increase in size over a period of time and are enabled to take in more blood and, in turn, pump more blood to the muscles. Obviously the time of the fast run must not be too fast otherwise the athlete will not be able to carry out a sufficient number of repetitions and the whole process will be erratic as the heart rate increases beyond the accepted 180 beats per minute. The training threshold lies between 140 and 180 beats per minute and at the end of the recovery period it should be down to 120 beats per minute. This type of training is far more favourable to the 5,000 metre–10,000 metre distance runner than to the 800 metre–1,500 metre runner.

Speed-endurance running also known as *tempo running*
This type of training accustoms the athlete to handling a high oxygen debt and an excess of lactic acid. This work is most suitable for the 800 metre/1,500 metre runner and, in particular, for the 800 metre specialist. The work consists of a fast section followed by a short recovery in which the athlete does not have time to recover completely. He now repeats the fast section still maintaining the short period of rest. This might be done in two sets with a longer and complete recovery between the sets, e.g.

4 × 200 metres (full effort) 30 seconds recovery
10 minutes rest
4 × 200 metres (full effort) 30 seconds recovery

Other distances can be used, for instance a useful session for 800 metres is 16 × 150 metres (full effort) 60 seconds recovery. The 150s are run very fast indeed with a rolling start and the slightly longer recovery allows them to be done in one batch.

Speed running also known as *repetition running*
Speed running is quality work over a given distance. The number of repetitions will be few and the recovery adequate to ensure reproduction of the speed. Generally the coach chooses distances nearer to the length of the race such as:

5 × 600 metres (7 minutes rest) or
4 × 300 metres (5 minutes rest)

Resistance running
This can be described in two ways – the first as running against the resistance of sand dunes, soft ground, hills, running in boots or a weighted belt and harness running.

Secondly, running close to exhaustion as described in speed-endurance running where the athlete accustoms the body to handling the products of fatigue.

GENERAL PRINCIPLES OF TRAINING

(1) Variety in training is essential and in order to achieve this a 14-day schedule is preferable to a weekly programme. Occasionally, surprise sessions introduced by the coach form a valuable break from monotony and a test for the athlete

(2) Endurance work must be done before speed work is introduced; in other words quantity precedes quality

(3) The intensity of training must *gradually* increase as fitness is gained

(4) Interval running on the track must be used sparingly especially out of season. A hard day should be followed by an easier day

(5) As the season approaches, work must be done at racing speed and close to the distance

(6) Competitions must be selected with care and with due consideration for the mental as well as physical condition of the athlete. Some competitions should be treated as part of the training while others should be of vital importance. In this respect athlete and coach must plan ahead

5
Hurdling

The three hurdle races for men involve ten clearances. The 110 metres high hurdles and 400 metres hurdles are regular events in international competition. In 1969 the women's race was changed from 80 metres to 100 metres and now also has ten hurdles. The 200 metres hurdles is seldom included in major meetings but is a very useful training activity for most events in track and field athletics.

Hurdling is a sprinting event over obstacles with as little interruption to the running action as possible. It is an exact event where a refined technique involving speed, extreme mobility and a high degree of skill is repeated ten times before the race is completed. One mistake and the competitor's chances are ruined when facing class opposition in the race.

In all hurdle clearances, whether for high, intermediate, low or women's 100 metres hurdles, the obstacles are cleared with a fast step-over action of the leading leg and a sideways action of the trailing leg, which is raised as high in relation to the hip as the height of the hurdle demands. The hurdler then drives at and across the obstacles, making room for the hurdles by picking the legs up and continuing the running action. This means that the centre of gravity of the body is raised only a little more in each clearance than it is in the normal running action.

In theory the take-off and landing distances on either side of the hurdle should be equal. However, since the hurdler is moving towards the obstacles at great speed, time is required to get the leading leg up and, therefore, the take-off has to be further away. In men's high hurdling, take-off distance is approximately 7 feet away and the landing 4 feet on the far side. In the case of the women's 100 metres hurdles these distances will be approximately 6 feet and 3 feet. However, as the hurdler picks up speed during the early part of the race, the take-off distances lengthen and the landings come in closer to the hurdle. Towards the end of the race, as the hurdler begins to lose speed, so the reverse occurs. The take-off distances shorten and the landings lengthen slightly, so the ratio changes but the total distance remains the same.

110 METRES HIGH HURDLES (see figure on p. 207)

The hurdler should take 7–8 strides to the first hurdle, 3 strides between hurdles and the run-in to the finish is generally covered in a fraction more than 6 strides.

The start

The hurdler should arrange his starting position to suit, first of all, the number of strides he is going to take to the first hurdle and, secondly, the length of the opening strides which will allow him to reach the first hurdle in the fastest possible time. If he requires 8 strides then the leg which is to lead over the hurdle should be back in the crouch start position. If he can manage 7 strides then the leg which is to lead over the hurdle should be forward at the start. Most hurdlers should adopt a medium starting position with a block spacing of approximately 16 inches. The distance of the front block from the line will depend on the characteristics of the individual.

Hurdle clearance

The following basic points of hurdling technique will apply to a greater or lesser extent to all hurdle events. Modifications to technique will have to be made for the negotiation of lower hurdles and different distances such as 400 metres hurdles, 200 metres hurdles and women's 100 metres hurdles.

The last stride before take-off is shortened slightly in order to put the hurdler in a position from which he can drive 'at and across' his hurdle. This, in turn, will mean that there will be forward rotation in the body as it leaves the ground and will continue throughout the clearance. This will help the foot of the leading leg to come to the ground naturally.

The leading leg must be picked up rapidly with the knee bent and reach its highest point before the foot swings in front of the knee.

The faster the leading leg comes up, with body-lean and drive at the hurdle maintained, the better the clearance will be. The faster the the leading leg comes up the greater the 'split' will be over the hurdle with the trailing leg left behind. The rear leg will then whip through late but fast and the hurdler will come off his hurdle running.

The opposite arm to the leading leg should begin an 'out and down' action as the leading leg comes up at take-off for clearance. It must begin the forward action early and go well in with the shoulder following. The other arm is merely brought back and into the side, bent at the elbow, maintaining as nearly as possible a normal running action.

Just as the hurdler should think of picking his leading leg up rapidly on the take-off side of the hurdle, so, as he crosses the hurdle, he should think of pulling his trailing leg through fast. It is better to emphasise a sweep-through of this trailing leg into the first stride on landing than a definite high knee action. However, in high hurdling, the knee does in fact come through high and to the chest before sweeping into the first stride.

400 METRES HURDLES

The hurdle clearance is a modified form of high hurdling technique. The vital factors in this race are the stride plan between the hurdles, economy of effort while crossing each obstacle and a state of fitness which will allow the athlete to maintain form over the last three hurdles.

The distance to the first hurdle is generally covered in 21–24 strides with 15 strides between the hurdles. The novice should attempt to master this stride plan, leading with the left leg all the way round. Some men with an average stride length of over 8 feet can take 13 strides for the first part of the race and drop to 15s for the last 4 or 5 hurdles. It is an advantage to be able to alternate, hurdling with either leg. In this case the athlete can take 14s dropping to 15s or start off with 13s and then drop to 14s. There are many variations and coach and athlete should work together until they find the most suitable combination. The hurdler who can lead only with the right leg is at a great disadvantage in that he has to stay on the outside of his lane throughout the race in order to avoid fouling with his trailing leg. This means not only running an extra 3 metres but also that it will be difficult to hurdle well round the bends without a great deal of skill and mobility.

WOMEN'S 100 METRES HURDLES

Since the race was changed from 80 metres to 100 metres, the consequent increase in distance to the first hurdle from 39 feet 4½ inches to 42 feet 7¾ inches means that most women take 8 strides to the first hurdle. The distance between the hurdles give an extra 1 foot 7¾ inches which allows women to take the normal 3 strides more comfortably. The old 80 metre race did not suit the tall girl who had to chop her strides between the hurdles and sometimes stretch a little bit to make 7 strides to the first hurdle.

In this event the athlete should concentrate on driving at the hurdle, a fast leading leg, body-dip before take-off, out-and-down action of the opposite arm to the leading leg and a very fast pull-through of the trailing leg. With 2 feet 9 inch hurdles a woman should do everything possible to maintain speed between the hurdles for the entire distance and develop a very fast pivot. In this way the sprinting will flow into the hurdling and the hurdling back down into the sprinting again without interruption. It must also be remembered that over 100 metres endurance becomes a significant factor and this must be catered for in the training sessions.

Coaching position (1) – at right angles to the hurdle 20–40 metres away

Common faults
  (1) *Not low enough over the hurdles and body too upright*
  Correction
  (1) Attack the hurdle rail driving at and across it
  (2) Adjust the stride pattern to the hurdle so the last stride can be shortened by about 4 inches. This will put the hurdler in a position of lean at take-off
  (3) Window hurdling – the high jump stands placed on either side of the hurdle with the bar at standing height for the athlete. The hurdler should then take the hurdle going under the lath. It is preferable to take 2 or 3 hurdles in succession in this manner
  (2) *Rear knee coming through too soon*
  Correction
  (1) Attack the hurdle and concentrate on rear leg extension at take-off
  (2) Faster pick-up of leading leg

149

(*3*) *Sluggish running between the hurdles*
Correction
(1) Fast pull-through of trailing leg as the athlete comes off the hurdle. Concentration should be on sweeping the knee through into the first stride
(2) Use the arms and drive powerfully between the hurdles
(3) Check that the landing from the previous hurdle is not off balance
(*4*) *Loss of form during the last part of the race*
Correction
(1) Generally caused by fatigue, so ensure that sufficient stamina work is done during the pre-season training period
(2) Training over 7 hurdles from time to time on a repetition basis
(3) Technique work when the hurdler is tired

Coaching position (2) – in middle of the lane directly ahead of hurdler

Common faults
(*1*) *Leading leg off line (i.e. not in line of run)*
Correction
(1) Ensure the take-off is not too close
(2) The hurdler should think of picking the leading leg up at right angles to the hurdle
(*2*) *Twisting over the hurdle and coming off line on landing*
Correction
(1) More body-dip
(2) A more positive arm action; the leading arm should go out and down early with the shoulder going in as well

TRAINING

Technique work should be done in the winter and spring whenever conditions permit; preferably this should consist of two hurdling sessions a week. Hurdling indoors is very advantageous if a suitable place can be found. Forms of interval running, resistance running, weight training, circuit training and mobility work should be carried out regularly. It is impossible to perform the intricate movements required in hurdling unless the hurdler has extreme mobility. Suppling work should, therefore, be part of the athlete's everyday routine. Sprint starting with the sprinters with the first hurdle in position should be done during the pre-season period and throughout the competitive season.

6

The steeplechase

The best material for steeplechase usually comes from the young cross-country runner who has also recorded a good time for the 1,500 metres. He also needs to be a rugged, rangy type of runner who enjoys hard knocks and hard work. The races are as follows:

3,000 metres steeplechase $7\frac{1}{2}$ laps (28 hurdles and 7 water jumps)
2,000 metres steeplechase 5 laps (17 hurdles and 4 water jumps)
1,500 metres steeplechase $3\frac{3}{4}$ laps (12 hurdles and 3 water jumps)
1,000 metres steeplechase $2\frac{1}{2}$ laps (8 hurdles and 2 water jumps)

Owing to the water jump having to be positioned either inside or outside the track, thereby lengthening or shortening the normal distance of the laps, it is not possible to lay down any rule giving the exact length of the laps or to state precisely the position of the water jump. It should be kept in mind that there should be enough distance from the starting line to the first hurdle to obviate the competitors overcrowding. Exact lay-outs for all distances may be found in the AAA Handbook or *Track Athletics*.*

WATER JUMP CLEARANCE

The technique of water jumping is of vital importance to the steeplechaser. If it is negotiated badly, it can be extremely tiring and sometimes dangerous; in many cases the athlete will lose a race which he could have won.

The take-off spot should fall between $4\frac{1}{2}$ and 5 feet from the obstacle and will depend largely on the speed of approach of the athlete. The

*By Bill Marlow and Denis Watts, published by Pelham Books.

athlete should speed up slightly as he approaches the hurdle in order to achieve a satisfactory clearance. It is better for the novice to arrange a check mark some 15–16 metres away and this mark should be struck with the foot which the athlete wishes to place on the rail. This will give him a 7-stride rhythm, the 8th stride landing on top of the hurdle.

Generally it is better to use the take-off foot for hurdling on the hurdle rail. In other words it is better to use the stronger leg to push off the rail. However, the complete steeplechaser would be wise to make himself adapt with either leg. It is recommended that:

(1) The ball of the foot be placed on the rail
(2) The body should be lowered, leading to a smooth fast pivot over the rail
(3) The athlete should reach out well with the leading leg off the hurdle
(4) The athlete should keep pushing against the rail with the foot of the driving leg for as long as possible. This leads to a good split and allows the athlete to be running as he comes out of the water
(5) The trailing leg (pushing leg) should be brought through high into the first stride out of the water thus avoiding any tendency to stumble
(6) It is preferable to land in about 6 inches of water and step out of the water on the first stride. However, lack of strength and endurance may mean that the athlete has to be content with falling short. In the beginning it is better to sacrifice distance in order to preserve energy. The uninhibited action of some of the steeplechasers from Kenya in clearing the water altogether is extremely tiring and certainly not to be attempted by the novice

HURDLE CLEARANCE

Since there are 28 hurdles in the 3,000 metres race, 17 in the 2,000 metres, 12 in the 1,500 metres and 8 in the 1,000 metres, it is of vital importance for the steeplechaser to become a good hurdler. Some good steeplechasers in the past have run good races by simply putting one foot on the rail and stepping down. However, not only is this a slow method but it is also fatiguing in that they have to pick up the speed of the race again on the far side of the hurdle. If they attempt to speed up the clearance by pushing off from the rail, it leads to a very heavy landing and this is not to be recommended. It is recommended that:

(1) The take-off spot should fall between 5 feet 6 inches to 6 feet away from the hurdle. This will largely depend on the speed with which the athlete approaches the obstacle

(2) The novice especially should attempt to keep as near as possible to a level pace. This will help him to consolidate his take-off spot. He should speed up the same amount each time he approaches a hurdle and rather lengthen his stride than break down into a stutter. This emphasises the importance of carrying out sessions of interval hurdling in training

(3) The athlete must learn to judge the hurdles correctly. The eyes must be kept on each hurdle as it is approached

(4) The form of the 400 metres hurdler should be studied and modified to suit the speed of the race

(5) Because the hurdles are solid, the young steeplechaser should have enough clearance to ensure the trailing leg comes through without striking the rail

(6) The athlete should hurdle with economy and as little wasted effort as possible

COACHING THE WATER JUMP CLEARANCE

Position (1) – at right angles to the water jump 20–40 metres away

Common faults
(1) Failure to judge the take-off correctly
Correction
(1) Establish a check mark about 7 strides out
(2) If he is already using a check mark, make sure he is hitting it consistently. If necessary, make any alteration which is required
(2) Boxed-in approach to water jump
Correction
(1) Group practice with several runners approaching the barrier at the same time
(2) Drive through with elbows out for a clear run
(3) Run wide and take the hurdle on the outside
(4) Accelerate to the hurdle to avoid interference from the rear

(*3*) *Stumbling when landing from the water jump*
Correction
   (1) Concentrate on acceleration to the barrier and keeping low over the barrier
   (2) Ensure the athlete is not driving too high off the rail
   (3) Work on obtaining a split by keeping the driving foot against the rail for longer and reaching out with the leading thigh
   (4) Strength training, particularly for the legs

(*4*) *Landing with both feet together and not running out of the water*
Correction
   (1) Keep the driving foot against the rail for as long as possible. This will create a split as in 3 (above) and the driving leg will come through in a running action on landing
   (2) Drive off the rail concentrating on picking up the knee of the leading leg and holding this position fractionally

(*5*) *Failure to clear the water jump*
Correction
   (1) May be due to lack of confidence. Practise over a steeplechase hurdle placed against the long jump or triple jump pit, then, when the athlete has become more adept at judging the hurdle and placing the foot on the rail, come back to the water jump
   (2) Concentrate on acceleration at the barrier and keeping low
   (3) Pivot and drive forwards and down from the barrier

Position (2) – on the track on the far side of the water jump and in the line of running 20 metres from the edge of the water

Common faults
(*1*) *Inability to position himself correctly and avoid the jostling of other runners as he approached the barrier*
Correction
   (1) Group practice over the water jump
   (2) Practise acceleration to the barrier and running with the elbows wide at that point
   (3) Practise a quick move from the ruck to the outside position in order to take the barrier free from interference

COACHING THE HURDLE CLEARANCE

Use the coaching positions recommended in the chapter on hurdling and study the form of the 400 metres hurdler. Modify the technique to suit the speed of the race and the rigid barriers.

TRAINING

Since this is a most strenuous event, the athlete must undertake a tough regimen of training which gradually increases in severity. The steeplechaser must combine the speed of the top class 1,500 metre runner with the endurance of the 5,000 metre runner. Ben Jipcho (Kenya) in 1971 ran 8:29.6 for the 3,000 metres steeplechase, 13:40.8 for 5,000 metres (having run the distance only twice before) and 3:56.4 for the mile. Therefore, fartlek, fell running and mountain climbs can play an important role in building up the necessary physical and mental fitness for steeplechase. Cross-country running is an excellent method of winter preparation provided it is supplemented by other forms of training directly applicable to the event. A typical winter training schedule might go something like this:

October–March 3,000 metres Steeplechase; aim next season, 9 minutes
Warming-up before every track session schould consist of 1 mile steady running followed by exercises for flexibility, particularly in the hip region. If hurdling is to be done during any particular workout then the warm-up should include some hurdling over the light barriers. Finish with a few fast strides over about 100 metres.
Monday
    (1) 12 × 400 metres (5 hurdles in position) 400 metres jog recovery
    (2) Weight training (separate session)
Tuesday
    (1) 3–4 laps to a 9 minute schedule. This is an essential workout for the novice in order to get the feel of the race and gain confidence
    (2) 3 laps in 4 minutes 11.0 seconds
    (3) 4 laps in 5 minutes 23.0 seconds
Allow 35 seconds for the run to the first hurdle to be added to the lap times of 72 seconds. The distance to the first hurdle, however, will depend entirely on the lay-out of the steeplechase course. This must be checked before commencing this workout and the times adjusted accordingly
Wednesday
    (1) Fartlek including hills (5–7 miles)

(2) Weight training (separate session)
Thursday
5 × 800 metres (2:24.0) 5 hurdles in position – 5 minutes jog recovery
Friday
(1) Steady run (10 miles). This will depend to some extent on priorities and the importance of the race on Saturday
(2) Weight training
Saturday
Cross-country race or club run
Sunday
(1) Hill work, fartlek or track session
(2) *Track session*

     1 × 1,200 metres (3:36.0) 5 hurdles in position
     15 minutes recovery
     4 × 400 (flat) 90 seconds recovery
     Alternative session
     Skill practice – water jump clearance

This schedule should be modified and altered to suit the individual. Its basic aim is to teach the athlete and condition him to the race with a lot of track work and hurdling. This should be done during the young athlete's first serious winter's training after turning to steeplechase from flat racing. Once he has mastered the race and has completed a satisfactory season, the following winter's work can be less rigid and directed more away from the track.

Summer – June–July
Monday
Fartlek (1 hour)
Tuesday
5 × 800 metres (2:16.0) 5 hurdles in position. 7 minutes recovery
Wednesday
12 × 200 metres (28–29). 90 seconds recovery
Thursday
(1) Hurdling practice 20 minutes
(2) 6 × 400 metres (62). 90 seconds recovery
Friday
Rest
Saturday
Competition

Sunday

Steady run 5–7 miles

If a gymnasium is available during the winter months good work can be done twice a week in the evenings. Skill practices such as hurdling and simulated water jump clearance followed by weight training can be extremely valuable. A beam and agility mat can be used for a water jump and two hurdles can be placed down the opposite side of the gymnasium (see figure below).

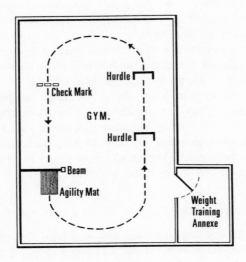

7

The high jump

The two most widely used jumps are now the straddle and Fosbury techniques. All other styles are either obsolete or obsolescent. The Russian style straddle is technically the most efficient jump ever devised and gives a longer impulse at take-off than any other method. However, the Fosbury is a completely uninhibited jump providing a vertical take-off and has the advantage of being extremely simple to learn, providing an adequate landing area is available.

At the present time at international level more jumpers utilise the straddle technique but an equal number of Fosbury jumpers, both men and women, occupy the top six places in major competitions. The club coach and schoolteacher should teach straddle in the early stages but may find that a few of the group respond very quickly to Fosbury depending on the availability of the necessary facilities.

COACHING THE STRADDLE (see figures on pp. 208–9)

(1) Skipping and hopping with alternate legs, the young athletes should be made aware of the leg from which they prefer to hop

(2) Taking long bounding strides, pushing vigorously away from the ground, the feeling of being aware of the jumping leg is consolidated

(3) Working in pairs, the take-off is introduced over a low cane held by a partner. A forward approach should be taught from a three-stride run. The hips should be advanced, the jumper being asked to run in with a pronounced heeling action on each stride, the feet landing well in advance of the body. The free (non-jumping) leg should be swung up above the low cane, having straightened

as soon as possible after passing the jumping leg. The leg from which one partner has jumped is tucked in behind the knee of the free leg as the cane is crossed. This exercise is well illustrated in the figures where the jumper is seen carrying out this practice over a higher bar into a pit. They should be warned that when swinging a straight free leg and taking off and landing on grass, they should be careful not to slip and fall on their backs. Once they get used to the timing of the exercise this will no longer be a hazard

(4) The same exercise is now done over a low bar into a pit, either a high or horizontal jumping pit, provided that it is filled with sand and not built up. The emphasis should be on a correct take-off, all movements being made along one straight line of direction avoiding any sort of rotation or lean. Notice the hips are advanced at take-off, the free leg swings high and the jumping leg is tucked in behind the knee in a frog-like straddle position, this being part of the lead-up towards what is to follow. The landing is made on the free (non-jumping) leg. When going for height, it becomes impossible to land on the lead leg and the jumper lands on the take-off leg which is dropped to the pit after crossing the bar

(5) The class is now asked to repeat the exercise, incorporating an upward swing of both arms. The timing of this movement comes easily when a controlled three-stride approach is used. Note the execution of the double arm swing in the figures on p. 208.

(6) The young athletes can now be moved to the track and shown how to work over skittles and canes or low hurdles, according to the age and ability of the group. These should be suitably spaced so that all can manage three strides between each obstacle; this will enable them to swing the same leg up each time they jump. They now practise the same exercise with a three-stride rhythm between the obstacles. Both arms are swung up together and the free swing goes straight along the line of direction of run. This can now become a regular exercise included in the normal warm-up period prior to training. It is recommended that the coach puts out six lines of three hurdles in order to cater for a full class with the minimum of wasted time. In the first instance the obstacle should be very low and only used after the class has gained confidence with practice over a low bar into a pit

(7) The class is now divided into two groups, the left-footed jumpers

going to the left of the uprights and right-footed jumpers to the right. In order to save time, it is best to use the long jump pit as well, the second group jumping from the grass verge. The jumpers now approach from the three-stride run, completing the correct take-off which they have already learnt thoroughly, p. 209 The turn, initiated on the ground with the free leg swing, takes place in the air and they cross the bar in the position shown in figure (b), p. 209. Note that the body is not thrown down into the pit but rather kept erect, back straight, chin in and hands clasped across the stomach. The jumping leg merely opens out from the position described in progression 4 and shown clearly in figure b, p. 209. The landing is made on the free (swinging) leg, as shown in figure a, p. 208. The advantage of this method of teaching straddle lies in the fact that at no time is the body thrown down towards the pit and incorrect movements ingrained

(8) This practice continues for some time until the coach is satisfied that the take-off is being completed correctly without any twist or lean. The bar is now gradually raised, the clearance being made in the same manner until it is well above the height of the hips. From this point on, technique work for the upper part of the body can commence and the clearance be made in the manner shown in figure b, p. 209. Note the position of the trunk which is lying flat, the flexed trailing leg opening out from the crutch. The jumper is not diving into the pit head first and the head and shoulders are not being deliberately dropped at this stage. The leading leg and arm are, however, correctly down on the far side of the bar. The landing will be made on the side and back

COACHING POSITIONS FOR STRADDLE AND FOSBURY TECHNIQUES

Position (1) – at right angle to the take-off and standing well back
Check
(1) Smoothness of approach run
(2) Position at take-off
(3) Free leg swing
(4) Arm action
(5) Body position relative to the bar as the jump commences

Position (2) – in line with the bar and standing well back
Check
(1) High point of the jump relative to the bar
(2) The body position over the bar (drape in straddle and arch as in Fosbury

Position (3) – in line with the approach run either behind or in front
Check
(1) Plant of take-off foot relative to the body weight
(2) That the athlete is jumping up and not leaning into the bar at take-off

COACHING THE FOSBURY TECHNIQUE (see figure on pp. 209–11)

An adequate foam rubber landing area is necessary before teaching this method. The rubber bed should extend well beyond the uprights on either side and be deep enough and wide enough to ensure complete safety on landing.

(1) Since the take-off is the same as in the old scissor style, the athletes should practise a scissor jump off a short curving approach of 5 strides. The start of the run should be slightly inside the line of the nearest upright so the beginner has a sharp curve throughout the approach. Let them get used to a scissor jump, turning in the air and landing on the back without a bar
(2) A bar should now be inserted above hip height and the practice continued. The short curving approach should be adhered to for the time being but a high pick-up of the knee of the inside leg (free leg) be encouraged
(3) As the athletes gain confidence in the back landings and the bar is raised, stress should be laid on vertical drive and a big arch of the back. Although the turn is actually initiated on the ground, it is good advice to tell the athlete that he must turn in the air after having driven himself straight up
(4) The coach should encourage the athlete after take-off to turn the left shoulder (for right foot take-off) back towards the take-off side of the uprights. This will help bring the shoulders square to the bar for the clearance
(5) The clearance is made with the hips crossing the bar in a high arch position. The jumper should be encouraged to have his

head forward looking towards the lath. The legs now begin to flex as the hips drop on the far side of the bar

(6) In order to clear the legs from the lath the body is jack-knifed the head and shoulders coming up as the legs straighten. The athlete now lands on his back on the air bed or foam rubber pit

(7) The approach run can be lengthened as the run-up becomes more controlled. The first part of the approach is now swung out and will generally commence roughly in line with the nearside upright. However, the jumper should come in on the same curve over the last 3 or 4 strides

8

The long jump

The three most important factors in the running long jump are speed at the board, upward spring at take-off and a good landing with the feet well up and forward in relation to the centre of gravity of the body. The most difficult part of the event is to obtain height after a fast approach and most of a long jumper's training should be devoted to this aspect of the event.

THE APPROACH RUN (see figures on pp. 212–4)

The total distance of the approach generally varies between 90 feet and 130 feet. However, some jumpers have utilised approaches considerably in excess of 130 feet. This means the jumper will be taking between 17 and 23 strides. The odd number of strides is sometimes used with beginners because they may start the run, hit the check marks and the board all with the same foot. However, many jumpers walk, jog or run on to a starting mark; in this case consistency of the early strides is very important. The novice might be advised to commence the run with the feet together toeing the starting mark and step off with the foot with which he or she wishes to hit the check marks and the board. However, if there appears to be tension building up in the run, it would be better to start with a walk or trot on to the mark. This method is conducive to more relaxation at the beginning of the approach.

THE TAKE-OFF

The jumper should have reached maximum possible speed some distance from the board. During the last four strides the necessary adjustments to the body carriage should be made in order to allow the athlete to make an effective spring and obtain height. This will mean a drop in tension, a more erect carriage of the upper body and lowering of the hips on the penultimate stride. The jumping foot is planted in front of the body weight and slightly towards the centre line. This will allow force to be applied against the ground for long enough and also directly underneath the body mass. As the jumper comes over the take-off foot, the opposite leg, knee bent, is swung rapidly forward and upward to gain momentum; so also is the opposite arm to this leg.

STYLE IN THE AIR

Once a jumper has broken contact with the ground there is nothing further that can be done to gain distance apart from obtaining a good landing position. Although the jumper can leave the board with forward rotation, backward rotation or no rotation at all, generally speaking there will be forward rotation in the body after take-off. If this is allowed to continue, without being slowed down or interrupted, it will lead to the feet coming to the ground prematurely and a consequent loss of distance. In order to assist with obtaining a good landing, one of two styles is used by most jumpers, either the hitch-kick or the hang.

In the hang technique the jumper swings the non-jumping leg back, straightened at the knee, after take-off, to join the take-off leg in an extended position. The body remains in this position until both legs are brought through together, bent at the knees, and then straightened and extended forwards for the landing. The first part of the hang has a hitch-kick effect as the straightened leg swings back and the extension of the body slows down the forward rotation. The arms are swung back, round, over and forwards working in unison and this also has some effect in temporarily interrupting the forward rotation set up at take-off.

The hitch-kick has become more popular with the world's best long jumpers in recent years. Here the running action is continued in the air, the legs performing either $1\frac{1}{2}$ or $2\frac{1}{2}$ running strides before coming together and forwards for the landing. The beginner will only have time to manage the $1\frac{1}{2}$ stride technique; the expert jumping much further will manage $2\frac{1}{2}$ strides before completing the landing. All backward movements of the legs are done with the leg straightened at the knee; all forward movements are made with the leg bent and snug about the axis at the hip. The greater moment of inertia of the straight leg moving back creates a backward displacement of the body, allowing the legs to come well forward for the landing. The arms generally work independently rotating forwards but some jumpers work them together as in the hang. Either way they have a slightly beneficial effect.

IMPORTANT POINTS OF TECHNIQUE

(1) Drive in at take-off, hit the board at speed
(2) A slightly bent knee position just prior to take-off
(3) An explosive jump upwards
(4) Trunk erect during the early part of the jump

Coaching position (1) – standing well back at right angles to the approach run

Common faults
(*1*) *Erratic approach to the board*
Correction
  (1) Adjust the starting mark and check marks as described in the triple jump chapter
  (2) Regular sprinting and low hurdling

(*2*) *Slowing down in the approach run*
Correction
  (1) Ensure that the approach run is correct
  (2) Ensure that the jumping leg is strong enough to work at speed
  (3) Put a flagpost in at 20 metres from the board and another at the board
  (4) Stand well back and time with a good stop watch. Check this time against the jumper's speed over 20 metres on the track without a jump
  (5) Insert a mark 6 strides from the board and make the jumper think of acceleration and drive into the board from this point
  (6) Correction (2) is very often the ultimate answer because a sudden increase in speed at the board will mean the jumper is without sufficient strength and skill to obtain height. This will mean re-thinking the weight training schedule for the following winter

(*3*) *No height from the board*
Correction
  (1) Corrections (2) and (6) for major fault (*2*)
  (2) Jumping off a short approach and bounding exercises with and without a weighted belt out-of-season
  (3) Drive up with the knee of the non-jumping leg
  (4) Accentuate arm drive at take-off

(*4*) *Completing the* 1½ *stride hitch-kick too soon and 'collapsing' on landing*
Correction
  (1) Delay the hitch-kick action off the board. Hold the leading knee high briefly before going into the hitch-kick
  (2) If the distance covered is in excess of 23 feet consider the use of a 2½ stride hitch-kick

(*5*) *In the hang technique, the trunk coming forwards to the legs, resulting in a poor landing position*
Correction
  (1) Emphasise a powerful take-off, hold the position momentarily and then swing back the leading leg straightened at the knee
  (2) Ensure that both legs are brought through bent and then straightened for the landing. If they are brought through straight, or straightened too early, the trunk will be dragged down to the legs in reaction

Coaching position (2) – at the end of the pit and in line with the approach run

Common faults
(*1*) *Swerving on the runway*
Correction
  (1) An unusual fault but sometimes evident with the beginner. Transfer the approach run to the track and have the athlete running down a line. This can take the form of 8 × 50 metres with a walk back recovery. Check each run from the front

(*2*) *Exaggerated lateral movements during the last three strides to the board, leading to loss of speed*
Correction
  (1) The beginner may be attempting to drop the hips deliberately

on the penultimate stride. In this case he will splay the feet and knees, passing through a position which is too low and so will lose speed. The correction lies in short approach work off 7-11 strides (not less than 7 strides). Too much very short approach work in training (3-5 strides) can often lead to faults being built into the technique, the lowering of the hips being exaggerated at slow speed and the limbs splaying to achieve such a position

TRAINING

During the winter months a strenuous building-up programme should be undertaken: this should include work for basic fitness and specific strength as well as jumping for height off a short approach. The following are suggested activities for the winter:

October–March
  (1) Fartlek (3-5 miles) twice a week
  (2) Weight training (3 days per week)
  (3) Jumping (twice a week)
Although it is important for the novice to learn either the hitch-kick or hang techniques during the winter, it is more important to practise jumping for height off a short approach of 7-11 strides. In the early spring the length and speed of the run should be increased, still attempting to gain height off the board. The athlete must not be discouraged after the first attempts at a full run and take-off. There will not be much carry-over from the winter practice until the jumper has had several sessions at the pit under good conditions.
  (4) One session of fast running should be done each week, 8 × 150 metres with the rest of the lap jogging to recover. If this is too much in the early stages then the session can be split into 2 sets of 4 × 150 metres with 10 minutes between the sets

Summer

Monday
  Technique work on the runway. Some work should be done from a full approach, and then, when tiring, some short approach work on specific points such as faults that had become apparent during Saturday's competition

Tuesday
  Weight training
  Some fast strides over 80 metres on the track or grass
Wednesday
  8 × 60 metres from blocks with a walk back recovery
  Short session of technique work if necessary
Thursday
  20 minutes easy running on grass
Friday
  Rest
Saturday
  Competition
Sunday
  Early session period
  Approach practice on the track with starting mark, check marks and
  mark to represent the board in position
  Mid and late season period
  Rest or walk

9
The triple jump

Whereas the term hop, step and jump is an accurate description of the event for the teaching of beginners, the term triple jump is more appropriate in coaching. Modern triple-jump technique has been developed in two distinct ways: the Polish or shallow technique which relies on a comparatively low hop and the conservation of speed during the other two phases; and the Russian method which depends on strength and agility, incorporating more bounce and height, particularly in the hop (first phase). Ultimately, the best way will be found by blending speed and strength to such a degree that a very fast athlete will be able to use to the best advantage a devastatingly fast approach and still be able to jump high on all three phases.

Although triple jumpers should ideally be equally strong in both legs, most have a preferred leg and this should be used for the hop so they work from the stronger leg twice and the weaker leg once. The technique of the event may be thought of in three ways:

(1) As an even rhythm which sounds evenly spaced. Standing at the side of the runway with his eyes closed the coach should be able to hear the even beat of a good performance: thump . . . thump . . . thump

(2) As an increase in height on each phase. Undoubtedly this is a sound approach for the complete beginner because the novice tends to hop too high and too far. However, this does not happen in competition; the centre of gravity is raised slightly higher in the hop than in the jump and the step (middle phase) is invariably the lowest

(3) As a spacing ratio for each of the three phases, with the ratio being: Hop, 4; Step, 3; Jump, 4

ESTABLISHMENT OF THE APPROACH RUN (see figures on pp. 216–7)

Conditions must be good, firm track surface, no wind and warm temperature. The athlete must be prepared and ready for speed work towards the end of the early season training period.

The exercise should be over 50–60 metres with marks placed on the track to indicate the start, check marks if necessary and the board. Normally chalk lines will do on a cinder surface but if a Tartan or similar synthetic surface is being used then coloured adhesive tape is preferable.

The coach or teacher must estimate whether the athlete is capable of reaching top speed quickly. If the jumper is of the tall, heavily-built type, who will tend to reach top speed later, then the number of strides in the run will be greater than with the small compact athlete who will probably have greater acceleration. The total length of run generally varies between 17 and 23 strides either from a stationary position toeing the line or walking and trotting on to the start. With the complete novice it is probably wiser to toe the line and start the run with the foot with which they wish to hit the check marks and the board; in this case they should take an odd number of strides. However, the coach or teacher must watch to see that no undue tension is apparent through the athlete striving for too much speed early on in the run. If this is so, then it would be better to insist on a rolling start on to the mark.

To begin with, using only a starting mark, ask the jumper to run through several times with a post at 50–60 metres. During these runs the coach should stand well back and count the strides, putting a series of marks on the track where the foot strikes the track on the stride he has selected to suit the individual (anything from 17–23 strides). After several runs with an adequate recovery, he will have established an average spot where he can place his mark indicating the imaginary board. He can now insert a check mark some 10 strides from the board depending on where he considers this to be appropriate. If the run is erratic, he can place another one some three strides from the start for the young athlete who commences his run toeing the line. However, it should be borne in mind that the fewer extra marks the jumper has the better – it is taking a long term view. Ultimately it is to be hoped that the athlete will be able to manage without any check marks at all. Some top class jumpers have only one mark some 6–7 strides from the board to serve as an indication and a reminder that they must drive in at the take-off from this point. The whole of the run previously merely leads up to this tremendous explosion of power at the point of take-off.

The exercise may now continue as part of the athlete's day-to-day training programme during the early-season period. The session would normally consist of 12 × 50–60 metres walking back to the start and taking an adequate recovery of about $3\frac{1}{2}$ minutes. This exercise will prove of great value to all the horizontal jumpers including the pole vaulter who will, of course, be carrying his pole. The club coach, assistant club coach or teacher can be of great assistance to the athlete by just standing well back, making careful notes and helping with the adjustment of the marks.

FUNDAMENTAL POINTS OF TECHNIQUE

(1) A fast controlled approach run emphasising an increase in leg cadence and attack over the last 6 strides

(2) The jumper should run off the board keeping the hop comparatively low and the trunk erect

(3) Attempt to maintain as much speed as possible on each landing. In fact there is a loss of approximately 4–5 feet per second of forward speed on each landing

(4) Emphasis on the foot swinging down and back on every ground contact, each take-off is then explosive and flows into the next phase

(5) Aim to obtain a wide split between the legs on each landing. This means the trailing leg can be brought through effectively to gain momentum

(6) In the beginning the arms will mainly be used as balancers and to some extent compensate for faults in technique. Later, as the athlete gains technical skill, they should be used vigorously to gain momentum

Coaching position (1) – at right angles to the runway 20–40 metres away from the point of landing for the hop

Common faults
(1) Erratic approach, inability to hit the board
Correction
See section on 'establishment of the approach run'

(2) *Off balance take-off for hop phase leading to marked forward rotation in the step and jump*
Correction
   (1) Look straight ahead and not down at the board prior to take-off
   (2) Keep trunk erect

(3) *Hop too high with the result that the leg buckles on landing*
Correction
   (1) Think of driving forward at take-off rather than springing upward
   (2) Ensure the athlete has sufficient leg strength

(4) *A short step* This is the most common fault to be seen in the club athlete and schoolboy. The best cure is prevention in the early stages. Sound teaching and adequate development of strength in the early days of a triple jumper's career will produce a balanced performance
Correction
   (1) The general cause is that the hop has been too high and the normal corrections are as for fault (3)
   (2) Keep the trunk erect at take-off. If there is forward rotation through the jumper leaning too far forwards, then the step can only be a recovery
   (3) Ensure that the athlete has an 'active' landing from the hop with a good split between the legs and drives into the step using the free leg and arms

(5) *Marked loss of speed after each landing*
Correction
   (1) The athlete may be attempting to handle too much height on each phase for his strength. Try a shallower technique
   (2) Think of landing flat-footed with the foot moving back fast

(6) *Poor landing at the end of the jump phase* This is a very common fault in triple jump because the athlete has lost a lot of speed during the hop and step
Correction
   (1) Ensure that the trunk is erect at the beginning of the hop. If it is not he will have forward rotation. A bad instance of this can cause the novice to pitch forward on to his face
   (2) Practise getting the feet well up and forward

(3) Try to introduce a hitch-kick or hang in the case of the more accomplished jumper

TRAINING

During the winter the athlete should incorporate weight training, hopping, bounding, giant strides and general exercises for strength and mobility from the beginning of the winter period. Much useful work can also be done in the gymnasium, such as bounding on and off boxes with a gradual increase in height, standing hop, step and jump practice and work off three and five strides. Also hop, step and jump testing one leg against the other. Do a standing hop, step and jump off the left leg six times and then repeat off the right leg. As soon as the weather permits, go outside and work on grass; this is preferable to a cinder approach at this stage of the training.

Winter training should also include fartlek twice a week with some short uphill work on steep gradients plus fast running over distances varying from 60 metres to 200 metres on the flat. Try to avoid the roads if possible because this very often leads to leg and foot injuries when carried out over a long period. Weight training is a must for the triple jumper because he is particularly prone to back, knee and foot injuries unless he is strong enough in relation to his bodyweight.

A typical summer schedule might go as follows:

Monday
Either a little jumping off a short approach or sprint-starting practice
Tuesday
10 × 50 metres (full effort) walk back recovery
Wednesday
Practise full approach run with a light jump. Some jumping may be done for distance if it is felt to be necessary but not as a general rule
Thursday
Low hurdling and light sprinting
Friday
Rest
Saturday
Competition
Sunday
6–8 × 150 metres (full effort) $2\frac{1}{2}$ minutes recovery

The pole vault

This chapter concerns fibre-glass pole vaulting for schools and clubs. Now that reasonable landing facilities are becoming more common there is no point in continuing with metal vaulting except where there is no built-up pit available. However, foam rubber is comparatively cheap and easy to obtain and most schools should have no difficulty in providing this facility.

EQUIPMENT

Before the advent of the Bantex pole the teaching of fibre-glas vaulting to juniors was impossible. Now many vaulters in schools are using fibre-glass poles with success. Proof of this came in the 1971 English Schools championship where nearly every vaulter used a Bantex pole. They cost less than £20 and are graded to cover vaulters weighing between 80 lbs and 140 lbs.

Before purchasing other pole vaulting equipment the teacher and club coach should check:

(1) That the stands are durable and rust proof
(2) That they can be moved forwards and backwards without difficulty
(3) The machinery for tightening the uprights will have to bear a considerable weight so they must be both strong and efficient. Generally the screws rust and the threads get worn very quickly
(4) Bar-raising equipment can be made quite easily by fixing a piece of angle iron to the end of a long pole. Two such poles will allow two boys to lift the bar easily back into position after it has been dislodged

(5) Vault coaches, such as Morton Evans (British National Event Coach), are using six-strand elastic instead of a cross-bar in training. This saves the costly replacement of metal or wooden cross-bars when they break

FUNDAMENTAL POINTS OF TECHNIQUE (see figure on pp. 218–9)

(1) The hands should be about 60 centimetres (2 feet) apart after a short shift of the left hand for the right-handed vaulter. In order to maintain a firm grip the pole should be taped both at the top grip and where the lower hand will complete its shift. A little venice turpentine should also be used at these points. A right-handed vaulter is one who grips the pole with the right hand on top, takes off from the left foot and swings to the right of the pole. The left-handed vaulter does the reverse gripping with the left hand on top, taking off from the right foot and swinging to the left of the pole. All further reference to technique in this chapter will be for the right-handed vaulter

(2) The vaulter must use a run at maximum controlled speed and give the impression of accelerating into the take-off

(3) He must develop an early plant of the pole. This means the right arm being pushed forward as the right foot completes the penultimate stride before take-off. As this is contrary to the normal running action it is a skill which must be learnt. An early plant is a fundamental of good vaulting

(4) He must drive forwards at take-off in order to achieve a pole bend and hold himself away from the pole with a flexed lower arm. The elbow must be in and behind the pole as he leaves the ground

(5) He should now stay behind the pole and tuck rapidly, the hips being held high. It is easier to tuck fast with the knees open although if the right foot strays too far to the right it will lead to a ragged clearance well to the right of the bar

(6) The vaulter should now go straight up, the feet coming close to the top of the pole. If he has swung up behind the pole he will have no difficulty in completing the vault. If, on the other hand, he has lost the vault by going through and beyond the pole after take-off, the feet will drop rapidly and he will come down on the bar

(7) The final movements of the clearance should be made with a

'thumbs in, elbows out' position of the arms which will hollow the chest. The left hand will come away from the pole well before the right but, at the same time, the athlete should attempt to keep all parts of the body going up while he is in contact with the pole

THE APPROACH RUN

The novice will seldom use an approach run of more than 20 metres in the early stages of learning to vault. Later on he should establish his run-up on the track by doing repetition sprints from a standing start with his pole. Marks should be placed on the track to simulate the start of the approach, check marks and take-off spot. Correct measurement of the run is essential and the measurement should be made from the back of the box when the approach is transferred from the track to the runway. The total length of run for the accomplished vaulter will vary from 120 feet to 150 feet. Most athletes will take between 17 and 23 running strides which might involve walking and running on to a starting mark.

Coaching position (1) – at right-angles to the take-off and well back
The further away the coach is, the better he will be able to see and interpret what is going on. Generally speaking the coach should stand between 20 and 40 metres back from the runway. At this distance he will get more of a photographic impression of the movements of the vaulter on the pole. The young coach should concentrate on one aspect of vaulting at a time because so much is happening at once and at great speed.

Common faults
(1) Unable to bend the pole satisfactorily
   Correction
   (1) Make certain his pole is not too stiff for him. A vaulter weighing 140 lbs would, in the early stages, require a pole graded for 135 lbs
   (2) Ensure he has a firm grip. Check this by putting a strip of white tape over the black where his top hand holds the pole. Any tendency to slip the grip can be easily detected in this way
   (3) Watch that the left elbow stays in and behind the pole and does not collapse immediately after take-off

(4) Try a wider grip on the pole
(5) Take advantage of a following wind on every possible occasion and make him drive in hard and straight ahead at take-off

(2) Upper hand slipping down the pole
Correction
(1) Use venice turpentine
(2) Check that the take-off is not too close. The left foot should be underneath the right hand (top hand) in the take-off position
(3) Work for an early plant

(3) Legs dropping too soon at the top of the vault
Correction
(1) After leaving the ground encourage him to think of maintaining his position away from the pole and keeping the bend
(2) Think of tucking fast and rocking back even further. The really great vaulters hold a position straight up the pole prior to clearance

Coaching position (2) – standing directly behind the vaulter at the end of the runway

Common faults
(1) Crossing the take-off foot (left foot) to the right of the line of direction as it is planted at the completion of the last stride before take-off
Correction
(1) Work for an early plant
(2) Drive straight into the pole

(2) Erratic run and inability to handle the pole easily
Correction
(1) Sprinting with the pole on the track
(2) Check the grip and his method of carrying the pole
(3) Read the section on 'establishment of approach run' in the triple jump chapter

TRAINING

The vaulter should carry out running training throughout the year. In the winter months this should take the form of fartlek and hill running. In the spring and summer, track work should be done and this should be a mixture of striding on grass and sprint training on the track both with and without a pole. Two vaulting sessions should be carried out each week throughout the winter, spring and summer. Only the accomplished vaulter can afford not to vault during the winter. Most young vaulters should be averaging something like 60 vaults a week or between 2,000 and 3,000 vaults a year. The work they do in the winter will lay a foundation for skillful performances during the following season.

Strength training and apparatus gymnastics are essential adjuncts to training for the pole vaulter. The strengthening work is best done with a carefully selected weight training programme with such additional work as rope climbing without using the legs, press-ups, sit-ups and walking on the hands. The young vaulter must be aware of himself in any position and, therefore, a high standard of gymnastics is very advantageous.

11

The javelin throw

Javelin throwers are to be found amongst boys and girls who have thrown balls or stones from an early age. In doing so they will have developed the arm and shoulder correctly for throwing the javelin. The shoulder must be supple as well as strong, hence the coach often finds that the boy or girl who swims well has the necessary mobility in the shoulder to produce sufficient range of movement to be able to pull along the length of the javelin and apply his force over a great distance.

However, there is a vast difference between throwing a ball or a stone well and a good javelin throw. It is an exact event and the skills of lining the javelin up correctly, running with the javelin and directing the force through the point must be learnt and mastered before success can be achieved. The coach should stand behind the thrower for the first month of the learning period, seeing that he produces a technically correct throw below maximum effort. Above all, this is a 'throw on the run' and, therefore, there is little point in practice from a standing position, even during the learning period.

FUNDAMENTAL POINTS OF TECHNIQUE (see figure on pp. 220–1)

The grip
The javelin must be held at the grip and the thrower should have one finger behind the binding, preferably the middle finger. It should rest in the groove of the palm of the hand with the remaining fingers wrapped firmly around the binding. Some throwers use the 'horseshoe grip', the implement resting between the fork made by the first and middle fingers. The advantage of this grip lies in the fact that the

javelin is held more easily in the palm of the hand and is more in line with the forearm.

The throwing position
  (1) The point of the javelin should be in line with the eyes
  (2) The head and eyes should be directed at the point
  (3) The front shoulder should be high and the arm folded around underneath the point
  (4) Both shoulders and the hand of the throwing arm should be in line
  (5) The weight should be on the rear foot with the knee bent and toes directed forward
  (6) The front leg should be nearly straight, heel touching the ground
  (7) Now the thrower should lean well back, keeping the point down in line with the eyes and tail of the javelin clear of the ground
  (8) The hips and legs are now in a running position with the upper body turned to the right

The approach run
The thrower should learn to throw off three and then five strides, the javelin held back in the throwing position with the arm extended and palm held high. The last five strides and throw can be referred to as the 'basic activity'. Later on, 4 strides can be added on the back of the 5-stride pattern to give the young thrower a 9-stride approach. The thrower will now use an overhead carry and learn to take the javelin back, keeping it in line, some two strides before the cross-step. On the 4th stride of the basic activity, for the right-handed thrower, the right foot crosses in front of the left, the thrower landing on the heel and outside of the right foot. During this stride the athlete gathers for the throw and the body is inclined further back.

The throw
  (1) The throw should be started early as the landing is made on the right foot at the completion of the cross-step
  (2) The throw is a long pull which begins by running off the right foot against the resistance of the left foot. The arm is not used yet; it is kept back completely relaxed
  (3) As the heel of the left foot contacts the ground well in advance of the body, the right shoulder begins to lift. As the ball of the

foot comes down an instant later, the shoulder should be pulled up and forward

(4) The right elbow now rotates out and up and the upper arm comes in, the throw finishing with a flail-like action of the lower arm

(5) Watch the point of the javelin at all times and throw through the point

Coaching position (1) – directly behind the line of run and some 20 metres away

Common faults

(1) An 'off line' throw, caused by the point of the javelin drifting out to the right prior to delivery

Correction

(1) Watch the point and keep it in line with the eyes

(2) Check that the grip is correct

(3) Keep the palm of the hand facing upwards

(4) Feel that the javelin point is over the head as the throw is made

(2) Falling away to the left as the throw is made. The thrower is bound to tilt to the left to some extent but when the left side collapses this becomes a fundamental error

Correction

(1) Ensure the thrower has sufficient leg strength

(2) Throw over a braced left leg

(3) Keep the left side firm

(3) Excessive vibration of the javelin in flight

Correction

(1) Ensure that the force is being applied along the line of the javelin. The thrower must watch the point of the implement and throw through it or direct the binding towards the point

(2) Check that the thrower is not pulling down on the shaft just before release

Coaching position (2) – from the side and at right angles to the throw some 20 metres away
Common faults
(*1*) *A 'bent-arm' throw, caused by anticipating the throwing action of the arm*
Correction
(1) Leave the throwing arm behind and 'run away' from the javelin
(2) Static practice of rotating the elbow 'up and out' against resistance

(*2*) *Running – stopping and then throwing*
Correction
(1) Throwing off a short approach run, concentrating on continuity the quick turning-in of the right knee and hip at the beginning of the throw. Then gradually increase the length of run maintaining speed and control. There is no short answer to this fault; it is a matter of steady practice over a period of time

(*3*) *Javelin angled too steeply and then 'stalling'*
Correction
(1) Keep the palm of the hand a little higher (in line with the shoulders) and point lower before the release
(2) The angle of release will depend on the type of javelin. Aerodynamic javelins should be released at a lower angle than the older type of javelin

(*4*) *Point not landing first – no mark is made and hence there is a 'no throw'*
Correction
(1) As for fault *3* correction (1) above
(2) Check that the aerodynamic javelin, if being used, is the correct one for the distance of throw

(*5*) *Failure to drive the right hip into the throw*
Correction
(1) Check that the left foot is slightly to the thrower's left
(2) Initiate hip thrust from a fast turning-in of the right foot
(3) Ensure that the throwing base is sufficiently wide

12

The shot put

There are certain fundamental principles which apply to all throwing events as well as shot putting. These fundamentals are the basis of all good throwing and the athlete must grasp them and keep them constantly in mind if ultimate success is to be achieved:

(1) The application of force over the greatest possible distance
(2) Using the strongest parts of the body first, legs, trunk and then the arm
(3) The correct timing of the throw so that each force takes over as the previous one finishes, ending in a summation of all these forces at the moment of release
(4) Working at speed and releasing the implement with the greatest possible velocity
(5) Having sufficient strength to master the technical requirements of the event

FUNDAMENTAL POINTS OF TECHNIQUE (see figure on pp. 222–3)

(Reference to a right-handed athlete)
(1) A controlled position at the back of the circle, facing directly to the rear with the toes of the right foot up to the rim of the circle and pointing straight back
(2) The shift across the circle should be low and fast, the rear leg extending in the drive and the left swinging towards the front of the circle
(3) The hips must get ahead of the shoulders during the glide and, on landing in the front of the circle, should be in line with the direction of the put i.e. facing to the right

(4) The shoulders should be facing to the rear, with the eyes focused on a marker some 3 metres behind the circle

(5) There is a tremendous lift from the rear leg as the knee and foot of the right leg continue to turn in and drive the hips 'round and up'

(6) The right elbow and shoulder should pass through a high position on delivery at the same time as the left side is kept firm

(7) On delivery the left leg, which has been slightly bent, straightens and contributes to the delivery force as the arm strikes

(8) The reverse or change of position of the feet, should ideally be made after the shot has left the hand but most powerful men tend to break contact with the ground fractionally before the implement has left the hand

COACHING POSITION (*1*) – *directly behind the athlete and some 20 metres away*

Common faults
(*1*) *Opening out too soon in the glide shown by an early loss of the back-facing position*
Correction
(1) Place a marker some 3 metres behind the athlete and make him look back at it until the last possible moment during the shift. Even as he drives up with the right leg and is lifting through a 'chin up' position the eyes should still remain on this marker

(2) Keep the left arm and shoulder pointing back towards the rear of the circle

(3) See that the left foot is being planted not too far to the left as it lands at the front of the circle. This is known as being 'in the bucket'

(4) Check the early starting position with the right foot pointing directly to the rear

(*2*) *Ineffective lift from the right leg*
Correction
(1) Check that the left leg is not 'blocking' on landing at the front of the circle; in other words, being placed either in line with or to the right of the right foot

(2) Consciously lift up with the right hip and extend the right leg

(3) Not getting the hip into the put. This is a bad and very common
fault with most young athletes
Correction
(1) The right toe must be turned in rapidly during the shift across
the circle. It should land facing back at approximately 45 degrees
to the line of direction of put and should be turning as it lands.
This must be emphasised by the coach
(2) Ensure that the hips are in line with the direction of put and
facing square to the right as the athlete arrives in the putting
position. If they are withdrawn and facing to the rear it is almost
impossible to avoid committing this error
(3) Check that the right foot is not 'blocking' as in major fault (2)
correction (1)

(4) Falling away to the left during the delivery
Correction
(1) This is generally due to lack of strength and if verbal correction
fails then positive action must be taken in the form of weight
training to make the athlete strong enough to handle the implement correctly

COACHING POSITION (2) – *for the right-handed athlete some 15*
metres to the right and at right angles to the line of direction of the put

Common faults
(1) Loss of backward lean during the shift
Correction
(1) Snap the right foot underneath the body faster, at the same time
keeping the body low
(2) A more positive thrust and lift of the left leg at the start of the
shift. Sometimes the expression 'reach with the heel for the
front of the circle' is helpful in this respect

(2) Speed of the shift being interrupted by pausing in the middle of
the circle
Correction
(1) Ensure the athlete lands on a bent right leg. The degree of bend
depends on strength. It is of little use insisting on a very low
position with a beginner who has little strength to pass through
such a position with speed

(2) Do not spend too much time on standing puts. These have their place in the training programme but it should be remembered that all throws must be made 'on the move' to achieve maximum distance

(3) Ensure that the athlete has sufficient strength and agility. The clean and jerk and snatch should be included in the weight training programme of the more advanced thrower

(3) Dropping the right elbow on delivery
Correction
(1) Insist on the right shoulder coming through high with the elbow higher still. At the same time the left side must be kept firm

13
The discus throw

The object of the turn within the confines of a $2\frac{1}{2}$ metre circle is to get the athlete into a sound throwing position at speed. The term 'running rotation' is used in modern throwing because the thrower should move across the circle at the same time as spinning. The 'running rotation' allows the feet to get ahead of the discus and a torque effect to be achieved. The athlete must be flexible because there must be adequate hip/shoulder displacement, the arm and discus coming late but fast into the throw.

FUNDAMENTAL POINTS OF TECHNIQUE (see figure on pp. 223-5)

The grip
The discus should rest against the flat of the hand with the fingers spread comfortably, the pads of the first joints just over the metal rim. The discus should not be gripped but rather be allowed to rest between the tips of the fingers and the first joints. The thumb should lie flat against the plate and should act as a stabiliser on delivery.

The turn
The thrower should face to the rear of the circle with his back to the line of direction of the throw. The feet should be about shoulder width apart with the toes up to the rim of the circle. Two or three preliminary swings are now taken with the discus facing downwards and the arm swinging at shoulder height. On the last swing the discus should go back a little further and, at the same time, the weight taken on the left foot. The left foot, knee and hip should be turned in the direction of the throw and the shoulders kept back. The athlete is now

in a position of torque, the hips ahead of the shoulders, the trunk erect, left shoulder high and the legs splayed in a bandy position.

The thrower now overbalances, the upper body getting ahead of the left foot. The left leg now drives, the right thigh is lifted and the athlete runs across the circle. This drive should take the athlete half-way across the circle, the right foot landing approximately on the centre line with the toes turning in rapidly to drive the hip through and up into the throw. The left leg must move quickly to the front of the circle, the foot landing slightly to the left of the line of direction of the throw and close to the rim of the circle.

The throw

The speed of the turn must take second place to landing in a good throwing position, with displacement between hips and shoulders and the discus trailing well behind the right shoulder. Hence it is better to control the speed of rotation and concentrate on landing in a position from which an effective throw can be made.

During the turn the right foot should be turning in so that when it lands it continues to turn and drives the hips round to the front. The shoulders should be back with the body weight over the right foot. The shoulder comes into the throw slightly after the right hip and the arm strikes from the low point, the discus being delivered in line with the shoulder. The discus should be squeezed out of the hand, each finger contributing a pull in turn and spinning off the first finger last. The rotation of the discus is vitally important because it gives stability in flight.

The reverse

The reverse will only be required at the end of a good throw when the bodyweight has been driven well over the front foot on delivery. The left foot is withdrawn immediately after the discus has left the hand and the right foot brought quickly up to the rim of the circle. At the same time the body is lowered to promote easier balance.

Coaching position (1) – in line with the direction of throw and 20 metres to the rear

Common faults
(1) Falling off balance to the left
   Correction

    (1) Make certain that the weight is decisively over the left foot as the turn commences

    (2) Think of running across the circle rather than spinning

    (3) Keep the trunk erect during the preliminary swings

(2) Discus going to the right in the throw, athlete falling to the left
Correction

    (1) Ensure that the athlete is not 'blocking' with the left foot; make certain it lands to the left of the line of direction

    (2) Keep the left shoulder up during the throw

(3) Losing the position of torque in the front of the circle
Correction

    (1) Keep the shoulders back at the commencement of the turn and lead in with the hips

    (2) After the left foot has completed its drive, move it fast to the front of the circle. Push the leg straight back; do not allow it to swing wide

(4) 'Scooping' the discus on delivery
Correction

    (1) Keep the preliminary swings horizontal and at shoulder height

    (2) Go into the turn with the discus at or above waist height

    (3) Throw with a wide swing of the arm

Coaching position (2) – 20 metres to the right and at right angles to the line of direction of throw

Common faults
(1) Losing the position ahead of the discus
Correction

    (1) As for fault (3)

    (2) Keep the right foot turning in as it lands in the centre of the circle

(2) Reversing too early i.e. before the throw has been completed
Correction

    (1) First of all the coach must be sure that this is a fault. It may be that the athlete has worked effectively and at speed and, in this case, the athlete may break contact with the ground just prior

to releasing the discus. If, however, the thrower jumps into the reverse before effective work has been done then it is a fault
  (2) Think of turning the right foot in rapidly and driving hard with the right leg
  (3) Standing throws coming well over the left foot on delivery and reversing the feet late and, at the same time, lowering the body-weight

(3) Falling out of the front of the circle
Correction
  (1) Ensure that the athlete is not moving too far across the circle in the turn and, therefore, working off too narrow a throwing base
  (3) Check that the left leg is well braced during the throw
  (3) Work for a lower position in the front of the circle prior to the commencement of the throw. Start low and move across the circle with control, landing with the trunk well back over the right foot

14

The hammer throw

Whereas the discus thrower is concerned with turning and running across the circle, the hammer thrower is primarily concerned with turning. He moves across the circle as a result of his footwork, each turn taking him forward approximately two foot lengths. Most throwers use 3 turns but some employ 4 turns. The latter involves some modification to the first turn in order to travel a shorter distance across the circle. This text will be solely concerned with the 3-turn technique.

The basis of good hammer throwing lies in:

(1) Having the longest possible radius of swing
(2) Increasing the speed of rotation on each turn, culminating with maximum velocity at the release when the athlete drives and lifts with the legs
(3) Acceleration into the turn so that the hips get ahead of the shoulders and the shoulders are ahead of the hammer. The hammer is accelerated on the downward swing, almost catching up with the thrower before he accelerates into the next turn, giving even greater speed to the hammer head. This procedure means exact footwork and precise balance so he may land on a stable base at the end of each turn

FUNDAMENTAL POINTS OF TECHNIQUE (see figure on p. 215)

(1) The majority of throwers turn anti-clockwise, the hammer handle being held with the left hand underneath the right hand. The left hand is protected by a glove designed for this purpose
(2) The thrower stands at the back of the circle, feet about shoulder width apart. He should adopt a sitting position with the knees

slightly bent and back straight. The hammer is swung back to the thrower's right rear, so the hammer head rests at approximately the point where the dividing line of the circle meets the circumference

(3) The hammer is lifted with an underarm bowling action and a forward and upward impulse into the first preliminary swing

(4) The action of the shoulders and arms are very important during the preliminary swings. Both must work to produce the greatest range of movement in the sweep of the hammer and flexibility between hips and shoulders must be developed if they are to be performed correctly. The novice should perform three swings

(5) Correct heel, side of foot, ball of foot action during the turns

(6) Bent knees and slight back lean to counterbalance and control the centrifugal pull of the hammer

(7) Acceleration from turn to turn, with each turn starting a little earlier than the previous one. This means that the low point of the hammer, in relation to the position of the right foot, moves slightly back i.e. in a clockwise direction

(8) Complete extension of the body at the end of the final turn in order to achieve an effective delivery

COACHING

From the rear, observe:

(1) Radius of preliminary swings

(2) Watch the speed of the hammer head and tightness of the wire throughout the entire throw

(3) The right foot should not be lifted too early at the start of each turn. It must stay close and low, travelling the shortest route into position

(4) Only the ball of the right foot should contact the ground at the end of each turn

(5) The knees must be kept close together while the right foot is out of contact with the ground

(6) The novice must concentrate on the footwork but never be allowed to look at the feet. This is the task of the coach

(7) See that the feet progress in a straight line across the circle and that they get progressively closer together

(8) Watch the left foot and see that it does not break contact with

the ground, even momentarily, throughout the preliminary swings and turns until the hammer is released

(9) Observe the flexion of the knees between turns. They must be well bent in a strong lifting position before the hammer passes the low point of its swing

(10) Throughout the turns the upper body should be erect with the shoulders relaxed and pulled forward slightly in the direction of the hammer

(11) See that the hands are well away from the body; they must stretch well out, particularly as the hammer sweeps up to its high point. The beginner tends to bend the elbows and pull the hammer in

From the thrower's right-hand side, standing well back, observe:

(1) Where the hammer head is as the right foot contacts the ground at the completion of each turn. The foot should contact the ground further and further ahead of the hammer with each succeeding turn. On the second and third turns the hammer should not have dropped below shoulder height before the right foot lands

(2) See that the thrower stays ahead of the hammer throughout the turns

(3) Maintenance of straight arms throughout the sequence

(4) Bent knee position between the turns

(5) Watch for any tendency to break contact with the ground. The thrower often tends to jump into the last turn

Coaching position (1) – directly behind the thrower, standing well back

Common faults
(1) Too slow into first turn
Correction

(1) Work more aggressively and with a wider sweep in the preliminary swings

(2) Throw the shoulders back quickly at the end of the last preliminary swing in order to catch the hammer early in its descent from the high point. Twist far round and stretch well back

(3) Sit back and stretch with relaxed arms, the hammer sweeping far to the left as the first turn commences

(2) Bent arms – a common fault with the beginner
Correction
(1) Push the elbows together
(2) Check the footwork and posture. Make certain the thrower is sitting correctly. Is he in position to withstand the centrifugal pull of the hammer?
(3) In practice place a track suit top on the ground to the right and try to hit it during the preliminary swings. Move the track suit further away and continue the exercise stretching out as far as possible

(3) Not moving across the circle in a straight line
Correction
(1) Practice numerous turns without using the circle and concentrate on the footwork without concern as to the distance thrown
(2) Check that the right foot is not being lifted too high or swinging wide into the turns. It must be kept low and the knees close together

(4) Loss of balance during the turns
Correction
(1) Continued practice on turns
(2) Check that the thrower is not burying his head and looking at his feet
(3) Check fundamental sitting position and footwork

Coaching position (2) – to the thrower's right and standing well back. Or, taking the back of the circle as 0 degrees, standing well back at 270 degrees i.e. the same position

Common faults
(1) No acceleration in second or third turn
Correction
(1) Check where the hammer head is as the right foot touches the ground at the completion of each turn (figure 19). The hammer should not have dropped below shoulder height at this point in the second and third turns. If the thrower is not staying ahead of his hammer, then move the left foot into the turns faster and concentrate on keeping the right foot low and knees close together. Arrive on a firm base between the turns

(2) Start less quickly and aim to build up speed more steadily rather than hitting top speed quickly

(*2*) *Leaving the ground during the turns, usually as the speed increases*
Correction
(1) Greater knee bend, check the legs between turns, they must be flexed deeply in a strong lifting position before the hammer passes its low point
(2) Improved footwork

(*3*) *No lift on release*
Correction
(1) Check for bent leg position. Knees bent, left shoulder dipped, left arm across chest and thrower well ahead of the hammer
(2) Work for wide final sweep of hammer around the left leg

TRAINING FOR THE THROWS

Winter training: October–March
During this period the beginner should do as much throwing for technique as he possibly can. It is during the winter months that the young thrower should lay the foundations of a sound technique which can be polished and improved during the spring and summer. There is no quick road to success in throwing. Winning distances very often start coming only after years of physical conditioning and technical training.

Owing to inclement weather and lack of indoor throwing facilities, young throwers in this country are often badly handicapped through the inability to practise their event during severe weather conditions. It is always possible to use indoor shots but javelin, discus and hammer present problems because of their shape and the distance they are thrown. However, nowadays a throwing net placed in a gymnasium can, to a large extent, overcome these difficulties.

When throwing outside in poor conditions, a bucket of hot water to keep the shots warm and clean and a numerous selection of cloths for wiping the discoi and javelins are essential. Hammer, discus and shot circles must be kept clean and as dry as possible. A hard broom and several old towels to soak up the moisture are a good investment on every training outing.

Strength work goes hand in hand with technique work because the young thrower must be strong enough to handle the implement he is throwing if he is to master the technique of the event. A thrower would normally weight train three times a week during the winter and spring, reducing to twice a week during the summer.

Mobility work is essential for the thrower and should be carried out daily. Whilst lack of strength is a handicap to the thrower, lack of mobility is also a decided disadvantage because it prevents the athlete from working through a full range of movement.*

Speed and agility are also essential qualities in the thrower. The distance thrown is dependent upon the speed of release of the implement. The ideal thrower should be big, fast and agile; in other words, not just big and heavy but more of a man who would make an excellent decathlete capable of performing a number of events to a high standard. It is recommended that the young thrower does two sessions of fartlek or general track work per week during the winter and sprinting during the summer.

Typical summer training schedule for 16–18 year old thrower
Sunday
　　20–30 throws working on technical points deemed necessary by the coach. Javelin thrower would throw with weighted balls, light shots or stone of suitable size and weight
Monday
　　Weight training
Tuesday
　　Main throwing session. Javelin thrower should throw at less than full effort working on important aspects of technique. 2 × 150 metres (5 minutes recovery)
Wednesday
　　Weight training
Thursday
　　Light throwing session or low hurdling and sprinting
Friday
　　Isometric exercises and mobility work
Saturday
　　Competition

*Those who require more information on this subject can purchase *Mobility Exercises* by P. R. Harper, published by the British Amateur Athletic Board, 26 Park Crescent, London W1.

Weight training

This is the commonest and most effective method of gaining strength. It is exact, easily measured and athletes find it the most satisfying way of carrying out progressive resistence exercise. The weight trainer normally carries out a certain number of repetitions of an exercise without a break. Then after a short break of about one minute he performs another set of the same number of repetitions. Part of a schedule for a beginner might read:

Bench Press 120 lbs 3 set of 8 repetitions

However, as the athlete gets stronger, progression should be made to use heavier weights with fewer repetitions. The athlete noted above might move on to:

Bench Press 130 lbs 3 sets of 5 repetitions or
Bench Press 135 lbs 4 sets of 4 repetitions

At a later stage he would probably progress to the 'Pyramid' system of training e.g.

Bench Press   130 lbs 4 sets of 2 repetitions
                135 lbs 3 sets of 2 repetitions
                140 lbs 2 sets of 2 repetitions
                145 lbs attempt (with assistance)

Coach and athlete must bear in mind that all weight training exercises must be performed correctly and proper safety precautions must be taken.

Safety

(1) Athletes must receive basic instruction on how to handle weights from someone qualified to teach weight training
(2) Weights must be firmly attached by collars and checked before use
(3) When specific safety apparatus is not available, the athlete must have others 'standing in' to assist when difficult lifts are being attempted

Once a young thrower has carried out a novice schedule for a while, he might undertake a schedule including the following exercises doing three sets of five repetitions in the beginning:

(1) High pull-ups
(2) Press
(3) Clean and jerk

(4) Squats or straddle lift
(5) Abdominal
(6) Specialist exercise directly applying to the event*

*For full information on weight training for all events refer to *Strength Training for Athletics* by Ron Pickering, published by the British Amateur Athletic Board, 26 Park Crescent, London W1.

15

The decathlon and pentathlon

Rules

(1) The Decathlon consists of 10 events which shall be held on two consecutive days in the following order:

First day – 100 metres, long jump, putting the shot, high jump and 400 metres

Second day – 110 metres hurdles, throwing the discus, pole vault, throwing the javelin and 1,500 metres

(2) The order of competing shall be drawn before each separate event

(3) In the 100 metres, 400 metres and 110 metres hurdles events the competitors shall be drawn by lot in groups by the referee so that preferably three or more competitors, and never less than two, are in each group. In the 1,500 metres each group should consist of five or more competitors. The referee shall have power to re-arrange any group if in his opinion it is desirable

(4) The IAAF rules for each event constituting the competition will apply with the following exceptions:

(a) In the long jump and each of the throwing events, each competitor shall be allowed three trails only

(b) Each competitor's time shall be timed by three time-keepers independently. If for any reason only two register times, and these two disagree, the longer time of the two shall be adopted as official. Alternatively times may be recorded by an approved electrical device

(c) In the running trials and the hurdles a competitor shall be disqualified in any event in which he has made three false starts

(5) The scores separately and combined should be announced to the competitors after the completion of each event

(6) The winner shall be the competitor who has obtained the highest number of points in the ten events, awarded on the basis of the I.A.A.F. Scoring Table

(7) In the event of a tie, the winner shall be the competitor who has received the higher points in a majority of events. If this does not resolve the tie, the winner shall be the competitor who has the highest number of points in any one of the events. This procedure whall apply to ties for any place in the competition

(8) Any athlete failing to start or make a trial in one of the ten events of the Decathlon shall not be allowed to take part in the following event, but shall be considered to have abandoned the competition. He shall not therefore figure in the final classification

Scoring is done with the tables produced by the Swedes in 1962.*

TRAINING FOR THE DECATHLON

The decathlete must work for a high level of basic fitness in the first instance. Broadly speaking he should train for:

Speed All the events require basic speed, in particular 100 metres, 400 metres, long jump and 110 metres hurdles but also such events as the pole vault which requires the athlete to 'attack' towards the end of the approach run. The ability to move fast is also a great asset in all the throwing events

Strength Progressive resistance exercised leads to power for sprinting, jumping and throwing. The decathlete should be a big, strong and fast man

Technical skill In all the technical events the decathlete must work to master the basic technique. It is just as important to work to improve the strong events as it is to eliminate his weaknesses. However, when he is technically sound in an event it will be a good policy to work 'a little and often' at this event and this will allow him time to concentrate on acquiring new skills

Competition The beginner should first of all tackle a few Pentathlons before progressing to the full 10 events. However, his first aim must be to complete the 10 events and score in each of them. Once he has done this, he is on his way to becoming a full-blooded decathlete. He must look upon this as something to be proud of, for this is the toughest of all competitions in the Olympic programme.

*These are obtainable from the IAAF, 162 Upper Richmond Road, Putney, London SW15.

The two most difficult events are the 110 metres hurdles and the pole vault and he may have to concentrate on these in the early days of his training in order to become sufficiently proficient to score satisfactorily*

PENTATHLON

The pentathlon events are divided over two days as follows:
First day – 100 metres hurdles, shot put, high jump
Second day – long jump, 200 metres
In the 100 metres hurdles and 200 metres the time of each competitor shall be taken separately by at least two timekeepers and if their times differ, the slower time be recorded.

Each performance is allocated a number of points set out in the Scoring Table for Women's Track and Field Events. These are obtainable from the IAAF.

The pentathlon does not present the same problems in technical skill as the decathlon. Most athletically inclined girls who are well built physically, fast and agile, are capable of making a reasonable attempt at the five events. The only problem lies in gaining sufficient strength to gain good points in the shot put.

Training

As in the decathlon it is just as important, if not more so, to perfect the strong events as it is to bolster up the weak ones. Hence 'a little and often' is a good maxim for the skills in which the girl is reasonably proficient, leaving time to master new techniques and, maybe, gain strength and agility for the shot put.

Competition

In the long jump and shot put make certain the first attempt scores. A 'no jump' or foul put on the first attempt will put the athlete under stress for the second and third jumps or throws.

The more competitions the athlete enters, the more experienced a competitor she will become. In the early days of a pentathlete's career the emphasis must be on gaining experience and not so much on preserving mental and physical strength for the major meetings. Careful planning of the competitive season will come later in her career when she is aiming for international honours.

*For further information on this subject consult *Decathlon* by Tom McNab published by the British Amateur Athletic Board, 26 Park Crescent, London W1.

Sprinting

Athlete should think about:

a	b	c	d
Bracing fingers. Straight arms. Forward position of shoulders Head in line with back Eyes focussed about a yard in front of hands Relaxation	Raising the hips steadily Taking a deep breath and holding it The action of running rather than listening for the report of the gun Maintaining the highest position of the shoulders by keeping the arms straight and fingers braced	Driving forcefully from the blocks bringing the rear leg through fast Keeping the trunk low Moving the arms vigorously from the shoulders	

Coach should observe:

Feet firmly against blocks
Shoulders already forward in front of hands and line
Knee of rear leg resting on ground opposite instep of front foot
Hands equidistant from the line of the centre bar of the blocks extended forward

Hips slightly higher than shoulders
Angle at front knee 90°
Angle at rear knee 110°–120°
'Flattish' back
Arms straight and weight on high bridge of forefinger and thumb
Shoulders in advance of the line

That the athlete does not jump off the blocks
Look for smooth acceleration
Vigorous arm and leg drive
Rapid action of the rear leg, the foot coming to the ground quickly, landing about one foot beyond the starting line
That there is no undue tension

Athlete should think about:

e	f	g	h

As for c and d
Holding body lean until 8–10 strides have been covered
Picking the knees up high underneath a low body; this will assist with momentum and drive
Vigorous extension of the driving leg

aintaining body lean
Opening out the strides as quickly as possible
Drive, drive, drive!
Pulling the elbows back
Relaxation

Coach should observe:

That the athlete does not 'patter' away from the blocks
The full extension of the driving leg
That the arm action is vigorous and in the line of running
That the athlete maintains a low body carriage

The strides opening out as quickly and economically as possible
Maintenance of a long powerful arm action
The impression that the runner is 'devouring the ground with the thighs'

Relay racing

Outgoing runner should think about:

a	b
Driving out powerfully	Staying on outside of lane (1st and 3rd changes)
Presenting a good hand, palm down, elbow slightly bent, wide fork between thumb and first finger	Keep accelerating
	Waiting for baton to strike hand – not 'grabbing' for baton
	Getting as much of the baton through in front of the hand as possible

Incoming runner should think about:

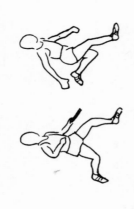

c	d
Concentrate on target	Speed out of box
Reach and sweep the baton up into hand	Have I enough baton in front to hand over to the next runner?
Getting as much of the baton through the outgoing runner's hand as possible	If not then squeeze it through palm of hand
Ensure the baton is firmly gripped by the outgoing runner before releasing	
If overshooting outgoing runner then shout for hand early and get the baton in quickly	

Coach should observe – outgoing runner

a	b
Athlete should not look round	That athlete keeps accelerating
Fast acceleration	Good reach back with hand
That hand is in position early enough to present a good target, palm down wide fork between first finger and thumb	Free distance between runners
	The athlete does not 'grab' for baton

c	d
That the outgoing runner stays on the outside of his lane	
That he has enough of the baton forward of his hand for the next change	
The baton speed is maintained	

Coach should observe – incoming runner

Maintenance of speed into the box

Shout for hand at the right moment

That the athlete makes one clean upward sweep and hits target firmly

That there is sufficient free distance between the runners at the moment of change

If there is any tendency to 'overshoot' the outgoing runner, check that the athlete appreciates this early enough to shout for the hand and get the baton in. Quick perception by the incoming runner can retrieve the situation if the outgoing runner has gone late or is running badly

Check that he stays in his lane until all other runners have passed

If the outgoing runner has not got enough of the baton through his hand for the next change then he must squeeze it through his palm. This can be done by rotating the thumb outwards over the top of the baton and squeezing with the fingers

205

Middle distance running

This series of pictures shows the normal relaxed action of the middle distance runner. The leg action is modified from that of sprinting. The leg cadence is slowed down and the knee lift is not so exaggerated; at the same time sufficient stride length must be maintained. The athlete will land on the ball of the foot and then drop back on to the heel during the supporting phase of running action. Although, during training sessions, over striding can be a useful exercise, if the beginner attempts this in competition it will prove extremely fatiguing and the results will be disastrous. An inexperienced runner can win races if he is understriding but seldom, if ever, by attempting to overstride.

The forward lean of the runner will not be as great in middle distance running as in sprinting. The amount of lean depends on other factors besides the force being exerted against the ground by the legs, and, therefore, it is better for the runner to concentrate on performing the movements of the limbs correctly and in time the body-lean will adjust itself to suit the physical characteristics of the athlete and natural method of running.

The arm action in middle and long distance running differs from sprinting in that the arms are merely used as balancers to counteract the movements of the legs. Note that throughout the sequence shown in the figure arm and leg work together. For instance in figure b, as the left leg is completing the driving phase, the left arm comes forward with the right leg and the right arm swings back bent at the elbow. However, all this happens quite naturally and the young runner should merely concentrate on swinging the arms sufficiently to avoid exaggeration of the shoulder movements. The shoulders should stay more or less square to the front in running and only move a little to assist the arms to balance the leg movements

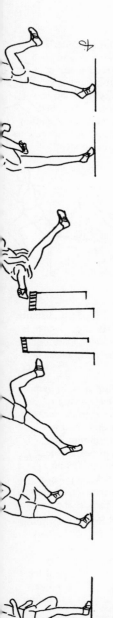

Hurdling

Athlete should think about:

a

Shortened last stride
Attack at hurdle rail
Stay high

b

Fast leading leg
Drive at and across the hurdle rail
Body dip

c

Out and down action of leading arm
Attack and dip

d

Pull through of trailing leg
Continuous running action
Maintenance of body dip

e

Coming off the hurdle running
Rear leg through fast and high into first stride
Use of arms

f

Hurdling flowing into running
Shoulders square to front
Positive arm action

Coach should observe:

Body weight forward over foot
High hip position
Check take-off distance from hurdle

Thigh of leading leg reaching hip height before foot
Foot swings in front of knee
Body dip beginning before athlete breaks contact with ground

Drive at hurdle rail
Wide split between legs
Leading arm and shoulder well in

See split and then fast whip through of trail leg
Shoulders square to front
Fast, smooth running action of legs

Lead leg coming naturally to the ground
High knee pick-up and sweep through of trail leg

Straddle (1)

An excellent practice which should be continued throughout a jumper's career. The approach is made at right angles to the bar with a 3- and then 5-stride run. Figure a shows a high straight swing of the free leg and a direct upward thrust from the jumping leg. Figure b illustrates the way the take-off leg is tucked in behind the knee and the landing made on the free leg. It should be remembered that these pictures only show the final stages of a practice which begins with a correct approach, the jumper coming in heel-heel-heel with the hips advanced in a forward position. All movements should be made in a straight line along the line of run. Later on a full approach will be used and the bar raised considerably

Straddle (2)

These illustrations have been produced from photographs taken of *Jaroslawa Bieda* (Poland) and show the correct method of teaching straddle. An efficient take-off has been taught previously and now the jump takes place from a three-stride run with the hips advanced

a The take-off position with the free leg swinging upwards, straightened at the knee. The take-off foot has been planted well ahead of the hips and both arms are working together, moving upwards with the free leg

b The turn, having been initiated mainly by the free leg swing at take-off, is completed in the air. The trunk is kept erect and not thrown down, the jumping leg folds up into a bent position and opens out from the hips. This is a similar position to that shown in the initial take-off exercises in straddle (1) The arms are held across the stomach as she crosses the bar

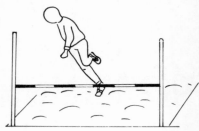

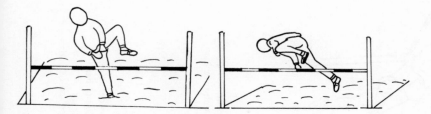

Straddle (3)

a The landing is made on the free leg with the body erect, chin in and head in line with the back. The jumping leg is kept in the normal clearance position, bent and lifted out and up

b The bar is now gradually raised until it is above hip height. At this point a complete straddle jump can be made and this is well demonstrated by Jaroslawa Bieda. Note that the leading leg and right arm have crossed the bar and are going down on the far side.
The body lies along the bar and parallel to it and the trailing leg is bent and opened out from the hips.
Landing is made on side and back

Fosbury (1)

Every training session should commence with a period of warming-up and preparation. When outside, the athletes should start by jogging and running round the fields, the coach introducing mobility exercises every 100 metres–200 metres. These should gradually increase in range and begin to simulate, first of all, the straddle take-off and then bar clearance and trailing leg action.

Much of the simple technique can be taught in this way during this preparatory period of 20–30 minutes. Small trees or railings can be used for support when carrying out high kicking and leg swinging movements. The above figures illustrate a simple but very necessary exercise that should be done during a warm-up period. Notice that the free leg is taken well behind the body before beginning the forward-upward swing.
Maximum speed should be attained as the foot swings past the vertical or, in this case, just after the right foot passes the left foot

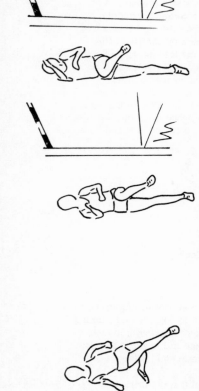

Fosbury (2)

Athlete should think about:

a   b

Smooth curved approach
Back on heels for last three strides
Lean away from bar on final stride

c

Scissor take-off
Explosive lift
Straight up
Fast bent free leg swing
Opposite arm drive

d

Turn in air
Left shoulder twisting back towards take off
Shoulders square to lath
Drive on up; never mind the bar

e

Hips up and extend for arch over bar

Coach should observe:

Curve on run
Final angle of approach
Plant of take-off foot in relation to body-weight

If take-off is vertical
That there is no visible turn before take-off
Forceful pick-up of left knee and upward drive of right arm

Turn brought about by curved approach and slightly rotational swing of free leg

Shoulders turned square to bar
Hips up
Extension of body

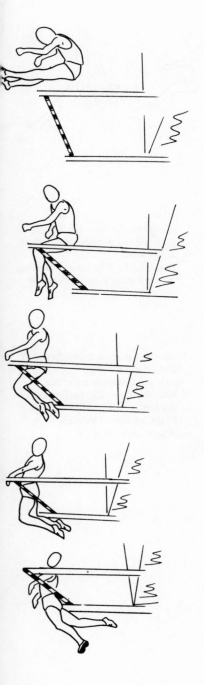

Athlete should think about:

f	g	h
Big arch of body and drape	Hips over, knees bend	Hold arch a little longer
Hips right up		Begin to lift head
Relax to extend		
Arms down		

Coach should observe:

High point of the hips in relation to the bar
Focus eyes on hips and see if they are up in relation to feet, head and shoulders

i | j

Jack-knife to clear legs
Head and shoulders up
Straighten legs
Relax for landing

Check clearance action. After the hips have crossed the bar the legs fold up, the hips drop and the head and shoulders come up
The body should now be jack-knifed and the legs will straighten

211

Long jump (1)

Athlete should think about:

a	b	c	d
Aggressive drive in to take-off	Driving up powerfully	Reaching out with left leg and then pulling it back straightened at the knee	
Trunk erect over last three strides	Holding spare knee high after take-off	Right leg folding up and coming through snugly under the hips	
'Snatch' jumping foot on to the take-off board	Delaying hitch-kick action fractionally		

Coach should observe:

Fast smooth approach	Explosive action off the board	Check that arms move forwards and follow the legs	
Slight dip 1–2 strides before take-off	Opposite arm and leg driving up together	Left leg straightened at the knee should swing back behind the hip	
Accurate strike at board	Athlete holding take-off position fractionally before starting hitch-kick	Right leg comes through snugly under the hip	

Athlete should think about:

e	f

Pulling right leg through and lifting for landing

Long straight arms swinging round and over

g	h

Left leg following right leg up and forward

Hold feet up

Arms swinging back and down and then forward and up as heels cut the sand

Coach should observe:

Height in jump

Smoothness of hitch-kick action

Arms circling forward either independently or together

Feet held high for landing

Trunk only slightly tilted forward as heels cut the sand

Knees folding and body pivoting over feet assisted by the arms swinging forward and up

Long jump (2)

The Hang After take-off, the jumper straightens the non-jumping leg, which had been brought up to hip level as he left the board, and swings it back and down to join the jumping leg which is left behind. His body is now extended in the air, legs trailing (figure d). The arms work together, first swinging back, then round, over and forwards. The legs are now flexed and brought through bent, the feet being held up and forwards for the landing

Hammer

Athlete should think about:

a	b	c
Pushing right hip round under hammer Pumping action of right knee	Fast close movement of right foot	Moving into next turn and relaxing the shoulders

Coach should observe:

If knees are close together If right foot flails or stays close as it should	That the thrower is not looking down at his feet That the right hip leads the hammer	Position of right foot in relation to left Right hip ahead of Hammer Hammer above shoulder height as right foot contacts ground Stable base

The triple jump
Athlete should think about:

a   b

Acceleration on to the board
Trunk erect
Forward-upward drive
Sweeping right leg back straight
Knee of hopping (left) leg being
brought through high
Right leg trailing with wide split
between the legs

c   d

Legs changed position in the air
giving left foot landing from hop
'Drive away' with left leg or
maintain contact with hopping leg
for as long as possible
Swing the knee up towards the chest
to give height
Wait for the ground to come to
you and then swing the leg 'back
and down'

Coach should observe:

Movement of the legs which
resembles the hitch-kick
Straight sweep back of the right leg
after left foot take-off
Not too high a hop for the
beginner
The hopping (left) leg should
describe a 'churning action' the knee
coming through in line with the
hip before the foot swings 'back and
down' to the ground
The trunk must stay erect

Right knee coming through 'high
and late' into the step
Lifting of the knee towards the chest
A good split between the thighs
Emphasis on height for the
beginner who will tend to have too
flat a step

Athlete should think about:

      e   f   g   h

Active landing
Drive out of step powerfully
Left leg swinging through fast and
high to gain momentum
Preserve split between the thighs
for as long as possible
Aim for height and a 'sail' technique
in the air

Maintaining split between legs for
as long as possible after take-off
For 'sail' technique bring right leg
through and up to join the left leg
Hold the feet high and give at the
knees as the heels touch the sand
Swing the arms forward and upward

Coach should observe:

The left foot striking the ground
actively and driving away forcefully
If there has been a good split
between the legs the trailing (left)
leg will come through fast and high
into the jump
The 'sail' technique will be all the
novice can manage. Later the 'hang'
would be preferable
Watch for any tendency to use both
arms and encourage the athlete
where possible

Good lift at take-off
How resilient the jumping leg is;
it may be weak
Landing with the feet well up and
forward. Lack of speed will preclude
an efficient long jump technique with
the feet far in advance of the
body-weight
Correct use of arms

Pole vault

Athlete should think about:

a

Acceleration into the take-off
Early plant
Firm left arm
Drive forwards at take-off

c

Holding body away from pole with a bent but firm lower arm
Rocking back and staying back

e

Rock back into 'kip' position
Hold hips high
Head back to assist with rock back
Stay behind pole

f

Feet to top of pole
Arms staying as they are until hips reach the top hand

Coach should observe:

Aggressive attack during the last strides of the run
Watch to see the right arm going forward with the right foot on the penultimate stride of approach. This ensures an early plant

Observe strong horizontal drive and 'hang' position behind the pole
Properly timed rock back with axis of swing at the shoulders

Right arm relatively straight. Left arm bent but fixed. The body must stay behind the pole
Hips go up rotating about the shoulders

Watch that the legs go to the top of the pole angled back towards the runway
Body extension straight up the pole
The legs must not come away from the pole

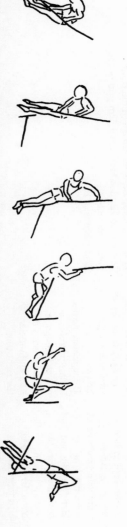

Athlete should think about:

i   **g**

Pull and turn late after hips have passed top hand and pole has straightened

Stay with the pole

Staying on back extending body up the pole

Stay back and wait

j

Thumbs in, elbows out, hollow chest

Keeping all parts going up while in contact with the pole

k

Keeping head and eyes looking down at box while arms extend

Head back only at the last moment after the right hand has released the pole

l

Coach should observe:

That the vaulter stays on his back as long as possible to obtain maximum vertical lift

Pull and turn begin simultaneously and should start naturally as the vaulter's hips pass his top hand

Watch that the legs are not dropping too soon

All parts of the body should be moving upwards while the vaulter has contact with the pole

See that the legs are not dropping too soon. If so this is an indication of serious mistakes made earlier in the vault

Javelin

Athlete should think about:

a

Short fast cross-step with hips down the line of approach

Keep javelin in line and the throwing hand high

Shoulders turned to right

b

Landing on heel and outside of the right foot

Body inclined back

c

Running off right foot on to left foot

Keeping on the move

Hips forward, shoulders to the right

d

Right leg driving the hips forward and upward

Left foot landing heel first and staying firm

Keep left shoulder going forward for as long as possible

Coach should observe:

From behind:
javelin kept in line

From the side:
Complete extension of throwing arm

Hand, javelin and both shoulders in line

Shoulders to right, hips forward

That the athlete has run away from the javelin leaving it behind

If the athlete settles in this position or moves through it

That he lands on the heel and outside of the right foot

If the right hip has been driven to the front

If the right hand is high and a firm grip of the javelin maintained

Wide throwing base

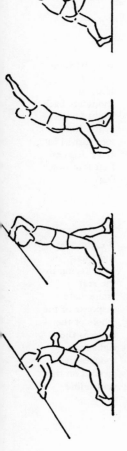

Athlete should think about:

e

Keeping the point down and punching up through it
'Aim the binding at the point'
Feeling the hand lifting the javelin all the time
Keeping the javelin in the whole of the hand

f

Tilting the head to the left as the elbow lifts up and over the shoulder
Release off the whole of the palm of the hand

g

h

Once the javelin has left the hand, the right leg is brought forward into a running stride
Lowering of the body-weight helps to maintain balance

Coach should observe:

From the rear – watch line-up of javelin and see the pull is long, fast and straight
Wide throwing base
Right toe drag and forward movement of whole body

Check that the thrower is not opening the fingers too soon and throwing with first finger and thumb. In this case the point will fly high

Check the reverse. If the novice is fouling the line it may be that he is throwing from a high position and off a short throwing base. Allow approximately one javelin's length from the left foot to the line of the throwing arc

Putting the shot

Athlete should think about:

a	b	c	d
Upright stance Looking back Lower body on to straight right leg and lift left leg into classic 'T' position Steady controlled movements	Both legs straight 'T' position Both legs bent, right leg bending as left leg comes in to meet it Lift left leg, knee back in, swing out heel (c)	Reach with heel of left leg for front of circle Drive off heel of right foot Snatch right foot across circle turning right toe in rapidly during shift	Eyes back on marker Hips in shoulders back Right foot on centre line, toes turned in at 45 degrees Left foot down fast

Coach should observe:

Relaxed upright position Left foot towards front of circle 18 inches away from right foot A balanced steady movement into 'T' position Shot into neck and outside rim of circle	Watch for good rhythm, success depends on control of these early movements Smooth, steady and exact procedure	Extension of right leg and drive off heel Good thigh split Low position maintained throughout glide Left arm and shoulder to the rear of circle	Weight over right foot, body facing to the rear Immediate response of the whole of the body as the right foot touches the ground on the centre line

Athlete should think about:

e	f	g
Keep eyes directed back at marker	Keep left shoulder moving forward for as long as possible	Punch out and up with arm
Drive hips up and forward with right leg	Chin up – look up	Right elbow high
Brace left leg and stretch left side	Lift right elbow and shoulder and strike late with arm	Right shoulder high Firm left side

Coach should observe:

Strong deep position
From the front:
observe full width of
shoulders throughout
the glide
Left foot in correct
position, neither
'blocking' nor 'in the
bucket'

Explosive lift and
rotation of body
Hips leading the
shoulders
Bodyweight coming
over left foot
Right shoulder
lifting – elbow high

If hip has come into
the put
Up and over action of
right shoulder
Body position in
relation to the left
foot on delivery,
lying back (fault) or
over left foot
(correct)

Discus (1)

Illustrates the classic 'T' position into which the body is lowered over
a straight right leg. From this position the right leg bends as the left
leg comes in to meet it and the glide begins with the heel of the left foot
reaching for the front of the circle

Discus (2)

Athlete should think about:

a	b	c d	e
Weight over left foot	Overbalance	Right knee high in drive across circle	Landing on bent right leg
Bandy position	Left shoulder up		Discus trailing
Turning left foot and knee in direction of throw	Drive off left foot	Turn right foot in fast in air	Shoulders back
	Move right foot fast	Drop on to bent right leg	Right foot turning in rapidly
Left arm and shoulder back	Run – do not spin	Keep discus high	Left foot down fast
Hip lead		Reach for front of circle with left foot	

Coach should observe:

Displacement between hips and shoulders	On balance position over left foot	Drive across circle, right knee high, discus trailing	Check position of body weight in relation to right foot
Shoulders well back	Hips leading	Right foot turning in	Is continuity of movement being maintained?
Weight decisively over left foot	Left shoulder high, discus trailing behind right shoulder	Fast movement of legs to get ahead of body	Is right foot continuing to turn in?
Trunk erect			Is discus high
Bandy position of legs			

Athlete should think about:

f	g	h	i	j
Right foot turning in Driving hips round Bodyweight back over right foot Discus high and trailing the right shoulder	Powerful thrust from right leg driving hips through and up Arm strike from low point of swing Keep discus wide and flat	Keep left side of body firm Press down with thumb of right hand Flat discus delivered high	Left foot back, right foot forward Drop bodyweight	

Coach should observe:

Body torque: Feet ahead of hips, hips ahead of shoulders and shoulders ahead of the arm and discus Bodyweight well over the right foot

Rapid turn in of the right foot and knee Are the hips being driven round and up ahead of the shoulders? Does the arm strike late from the low point of the swing?

Delivery in line with the shoulder Flat discus driven high spinning off first finger Height obtained from leg drive

Check athlete is not breaking contact with ground too soon If the throwing base is short sometimes both feet come off the ground together If wide base is used then the 'reverse' will be slower and more orthodox